IN THE
SPIRIT

IN THE
SPIRIT

Reflections on Everyday Grace 

NIMBUS
PUBLISHING
nimbus.ca

MONICA GRAHAM

Nimbus Publishing Limited

3731 Mackintosh St, Halifax, NS B3K 5A5

(902) 455-4286 nimbus.ca

Printed and bound in Canada

NB1177

Cover image: Colleen MacIsaac, *Winter Skies* (2013)
Interior illustrations: Colleen MacIsaac (2015)
Design: Heather Bryan

Morning Resolve prayer, p. 135, is reprinted with permission by Forward Movement, a ministry of the Episcopal Church. Learn more: www.forwardmovement.org.

Library and Archives Canada Cataloguing in Publication

Graham, Monica, 1954-, author
In the spirit : reflections on everyday grace / Monica Graham.

First published in the Chronicle-Herald newspaper column of the same name, In the Spirit.

Issued in print and electronic formats.
ISBN 978-1-77108-275-4 (pbk.).—ISBN 978-1-77108-276-1 (html)

1. Spirituality. 2. Spiritual life. I. Title.
BL624.G725 2015   204   C2015-900251-6
                           C2015-900252-4

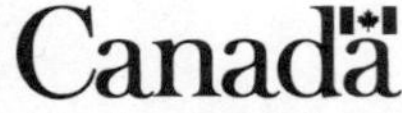

Nimbus Publishing acknowledges the financial support for its publishing activities from the Government of Canada through the Canada Book Fund (CBF) and the Canada Council for the Arts, and from the Province of Nova Scotia through Film & Creative Industries Nova Scotia. We are pleased to work in partnership with Film & Creative Industries Nova Scotia to develop and promote our creative industries for the benefit of all Nova Scotians.

To Mom and Dad

CONTENTS

INTRODUCTION: *Bokeh*

Bokeh is a term used in photography to refer to the out-of-focus parts of a photograph. It comes from the Japanese word *boke*, meaning blur, fuzziness, dizziness, or confusion. "Good" bokeh adds to a positive overall perception of an image, while "bad" bokeh distracts the eye in a negative way. When I applied in 2005 to be a columnist for the *Halifax Chronicle Herald*'s religion page, my ambition was to pick away at the unfocused bits and pieces in the background of our lives that make up our faith, religion, or spirituality. Like bokeh in a photo, life's blurry background goes unnoticed unless it's either really good or really bad; instead, the out-in-front subject of the moment garners all the attention. I got the job, so every second Saturday for eight years readers opened the *Herald*'s religion page to see In the Spirit: my musings, rants, and comments on faith-related topics—including some that I connected only by feats of imagination. My approach was based on three beliefs.

Firstly, I believed, and still do, that my opinions about anything, including religion, were just as valuable as those of anyone else with access to the same information. However, as a journalist, ethics demanded that I set aside any personal bias when researching and writing news stories. A reporter's task is to deliver the news, not to theorize or offer opinions. During those years of fence-sitting I quietly pondered all kinds of topics, but I arrived at few conclusions. I generally learned that the world's issues are not black and white, but consist of multicoloured shades that make up the backdrop of our ordinary lives. Spirituality and religion fit the same profile: a muddled, mottled, and oft-ignored background to important and obvious world, community, and personal events. The column would examine the points of spiritual colour and light that make up the bokeh of everyday life, and examine their place in the larger picture.

Secondly, I have an old-fashioned belief in vocation, that everyone has a purpose on Earth that will ultimately contribute to the greater good. Lucky people learn their vocation early enough in life to act on it, and the luckier ones get paid for it. My vocation lay not in cooking or sports or fashion modelling or nursing or accounting (all of which I contemplated). But I could write. I wanted to write, and I believed my words might help make the world a better place.

My third reason for tackling a religion column is the adage that writers should write about what they know. I grew up in a Christian household where theology was served with the peas at dinner. Family discussion topics ranged from the merits of parochial schools to St. Paul's views on women; from the motives of the knights of the Crusades to symbolism in *The Lion, the Witch and the Wardrobe*; from whether or not aliens built the pyramids to the role of modern music in worship. These were just a few of the topics hashed out over the kitchen table. What we didn't know or understand we were dispatched to research, a task that sometimes kept us up all night scouring the *Encyclopedia Britannica* or the *Abingdon Bible Commentary*. At school, scripture was a recognized subject, and our compulsory geography and history classes included the study of comparative religions.

None of the aforementioned points makes me an expert in religion or faith, of course. In fact, if the church bigwigs knew my thoughts on official teachings, they might kick me out.

Excommunicate me. Shun me, or whatever it's called. But it's okay that God knows my thoughts, because God knows me better than I know myself. If he—or she—doesn't like what I'm thinking, God will forgive me and coax me to change, although maybe not in that order. But the church, no matter how good, is not the same as God, is not always right, and is in no position to judge me or my relationship with God. While I am no expert on religion, I can claim plenty of experience in discussing the topic. Life experience persuades me that the human spirit is both tough and tender, and that something divine exists. I am certain that spirituality is one of the most important aspects of humanity and worthy of discussion.

The positive response to In the Spirit continued even after a newspaper redesign saw both the column and the religion page cancelled in early 2013. Readers said the cancellation was a sign of the times, but those times had long been signalled by the relegation of so-called religious topics to the back pages. Even so, religion permeates every aspect of our lives—just look at the front pages. Hard-news, front-page stories are almost all about human perceptions of right and wrong, and the conflict among these perceptions. We read stories about people hating and killing in the name of religion, people of deep faith putting their lives at risk to help others, victims forgiving their oppressors, and the profound spirituality of the wise. We are attracted to stories of sinners who turn their lives 180 degrees, of eerie coincidences that appear engineered by a master designer, and of miracles involving angels, healing, or even Jesus's image on a slice of toast. Humans are fascinated with the meaning of life and afterlife, and the lucky loonie at centre ice. These are all aspects of what we believe.

Call it religion.

Religion influences fashion and home-decorating pages: steel crucifixes and dragon tattoos, turbans on ladies at tea parties, and pews as kitchen benches. Food and recipe pages follow religious seasons and festivals: Christmas turkey, the Passover Seder meal, mathiya at Diwali, eggs at Easter/spring equinox, lamb for Id al-Fitr, and so on. Religion is everywhere. Everything we read, do, or say is coloured by the sense of a being or system beyond our understanding. This "Something" orders the world, so our actions have built-in consequences even when we don't know what they are. I'll call this being or system "God." Our profound sense of God is our spiritual life, which is disconnected enough from our daily grind in that it transcends ordinary life and will continue to exist after we stop breathing. This is the mystery of life after death.

Whether our belief system is deeply complicated, as simple as checking the newspaper horoscope, or as strange—to most North Americans—as casting chicken entrails, we all share the basic elements of religion. Even those who claim to have no spiritual beliefs oppose the concept of a divinity with religious fervor. They vow to guide their lives by concepts in which they have faith: intelligence, science, innate wisdom, or personal experience. We all want answers to the cosmic questions of creation, the mystery and holiness of the supernatural, good and evil: How should we behave? Why do we suffer? Where did we come from? Where are we going? What is important? These questions are part of the bokeh, the out-of-focus and influential background—but not the back pages—of our lives.

Writing more than two hundred articles in those eight years involved poking around places of worship, universities, libraries, and websites; consulting books, my intellectual superiors, and children; observing people, nature, and events. I learned a lot, and my experience is perhaps summed up best by astronomer Carl Sagan, who said, "Somewhere, something incredible is waiting to be known." I tried to portray in my column that sense of standing on the edge of discovering spirit, soul, hope, wonder, awe, faith, love; subjects that we can't reach out and touch, but that touch us every day. Readers responded with valuable information and insight into their own spirituality, and shared with me their deepest heartbreaks and their greatest joys. They opened my eyes, challenged my viewpoints, exhilarated me, infuriated me, and forced me to grow in my own faith.

And they told me to turn the columns into a book.

In the newspaper business, it's said that for every person who writes a letter on a topic, ten more feel the same way but don't pick up a pen. This was a good enough reason to compile some of the columns from those eight years, and to write some new material as well.

This is the book.

PART I

Marvellous Creation

CREATION'S DRAMA

Lightning, floods, earthquakes, tornadoes, blizzards, ice storms: when nature plays drama queen, we stand in awe (and awareness) of our own insignificance before the oh-so-obvious power of the world unfolding. Rainbows, the northern lights, shooting stars, a green shoot poking through fire-blackened ground: these are equally powerful images, though less destructive. Our personal dramas include birth, our first step, our first day of school, graduation, employment, marriage, children, and onward through conflicts, challenges, events, and achievements until our last great adventure: death. These are the moments we record in journals, with our cameras, and in the stories we tell one another. These are the times that we not only remember, but often find hard to forget.

In between the miracles, the world does not stand still. Each dramatic moment develops from the apparent calm that preceded it.

An ordinary drop of rain measures, at a guess, less than half a teaspoon of water. But several boring, dreary days of rain can add up to frightening floods. Lightning is preceded by an almost imperceptible buildup of electrical energy, and earthquakes by steadily increasing pressure along Earth's fault lines. Reduced to mere science, a rainbow is our rather complicated perception of light shining through water droplets at a certain angle. Thousands of tiny cells must divide, and divide again, out of sight, underground, before a plant sticks its green head through the mud. The miracle of human birth is usually preceded by love between two individuals, followed by nine months of gestation that, for many, includes days of vomiting and fatigue—considerably un-pretty and potentially miserable. A child's first step reminds parents that this suddenly independent being has been quietly gaining the strength and balance to stand on his or her own two feet. Graduating from high school, college, or university is a milestone that offers proof of years of studying and absorbing knowledge, a daily grind that many students think, at the time, they would like to escape. But there is no shortcut to knowledge, or a flood, or an earthquake, or new life.

We humans try to imitate nature by producing our own miracles, but the details are overwhelming and the results can be rather ho-hum. For instance, near my home, fishers periodically release into the sea two buckets of baby lobsters hatched in captivity in an attempt to increase the future population. The task is the result of years of research into habitat, growth cycles, and other lobster life tidbits. While it is an interesting project, watching the babies go to their new homes under the sea is a bit like watching paint dry. Miracle? What miracle? Similarly, a bone marrow transplant is a medical breakthrough, but recipients can sit and play cards while the life-giving stuff drips into them and finds its way through the bloodstream to the insides of their bones, where it starts to grow. On the surface this event appears incredibly un-incredible, and nowhere near as dramatic as a simple thunderstorm.

We are accustomed to turning a key and starting an engine, something so mundane that few people think of it as a powerful example of nature at work (especially since we vilify internal combustion motors as agents of pollution). But what about the circumstances that must exist for that turn of the key to set off an amazing chain of events that can move us at incredible speeds? The fact that we humans can tap into that potential is cool to the nth degree, but we didn't create or invent the engine from scratch. First there had to be a process in nature that sparks a fuel source, as well as laws of motion and energy, materials for building the machinery, and the human intelligence to carry out the project. Engines weren't just plucked out of nothing by someone who didn't want to walk to the store one day.

We gape in awe at the results of our own human handiwork and ignore that which is truly awesome: a world for which we can take no credit, a world which allows these human advances in scientific understanding.

It is so easy to overlook the wonders that hum along in the background.

AWE AND MYSTERY

We humans think we're pretty smart. We can send people and dogs to outer space, replicate DNA, make replacement body parts, capture the power of the sun and wind, cure once-dreaded diseases, and send silly and serious instantaneous messages around the globe. Every generation thinks it has one-upped the last one when it comes to the intelligence department—a notion reinforced every few years by a new discovery or scientific breakthrough.

From the wheel, fire, and inclined plane all the way to mini-microchips, quarks, and sound- and light-bending technology, those alive today have accumulated the shared knowledge of the ages. Possibly as a result, the average human now lives longer, comes in a larger size, and travels farther and more often than that of previous generations. But does this mean we are smarter than our ancestors were thousands of years ago? My efforts at cloning a sheep, for instance, would have no better result than those of a cavewoman. My vocabulary might be much more extensive than hers, and my clothing may be made from petroleum products instead of animal skins, but neither language nor polyester were my personal invention or discovery. Am I, or is anyone else, smarter than this long-ago woman?

After thousands of years of progress, humans still need the same things: adequate food and water, shelter and clothing, and human contact. Send any one of us as a baby back to a first-century village, and our chance of survival would be no more certain than the next person's. Time travel a healthy baby from Moses's day to the present, and that child's chances would be equal to those of his or her twenty-first-century peers. Just as it is in science, consumer knowledge, and culture, so it is in religion: we are no better than our distant ancestors.

Sure, today's religious groups exhibit signs of modernity. Architecturally, the buildings used for worship have evolved from simple outdoor or domestic meeting places to structures that, through elaborate decoration or deceptively simple design, embrace the traditions of the era in which they were built. The people who worship in these spaces may use contemporary language or slang. They may read from a scroll, a book, or an electronic screen. They may have traded beeswax for long-burning oil lamps or solar-powered LED bulbs. Music may be generated by a pump organ, a rock band, a computer, or a choir. Art Deco synagogues, mosques with in-floor heating and solar panels, churches with fold-up theatre-style cloth seats, and temples with musical fountains: today's rituals might be unrecognizable to a faith's first practitioners. But strip away all the trappings and language and rituals, and we discover a collective human yearning to connect with something bigger and better and smarter than us.

Call it The Divine, call it God, but it's something that can order the world and take care of us when our puny human efforts fail, as they inevitably do. Throughout history, that yearning has been organized into separate factions aligned with nationality, geography, wealth, and power, each with rules that promote distinctly petty and short-sighted ideals and substitute ritual for reality. It's the kind of stuff that gives religion a bad name. But however bad it ever gets, humans everywhere still seek that Something.

Therein lies a miracle: as different and separate, as contrary and oppositional as we are, we are created with a spark that makes us more than the sum of our physiological parts. We are still not as smart as we think we are, but the creation of us is worth celebrating.

THE WONDER OF US

Look at a hand. All those bones and joints and muscles and gristly bits and skin and blood vessels and nerves, which, under normal conditions, all work together to do things without us even thinking about it. We use our hands for good and evil, to touch and feel, to strike and stroke, to grasp and release, to give and take. They may be calloused, crooked, smooth, strong, delicate, rough, torn, agile, or stiff. And each has its own unique set of fingerprints.

Hands are quite marvellous miracles of engineering. But we have had hands since we have been humans, so mostly they are no big deal. We take them for granted, unless we lose the use of them. The same goes for our eyes: they have such shiny, clear, fragile surfaces, with so much going on in the background. If you had never seen or heard of an eye, and were told to build something that could sense colour and shape and distance and size and motion and relay that information to our brains, would you ever think to build an eye? All by yourself, could you imagine such a feature? Would you think to make it in so many beautiful colours and shapes and sizes? Would you surround it with lashes and brows and lids, which could be twitched with tiny muscles to send messages across a room without us ever opening our mouths?

And what about our mouths? Or, for that matter, our noses? Or our ears? I've always marvelled at how our ears and noses seem specifically designed for holding eyeglasses. Sure, if these appendages weren't there we'd just have to find another way to fasten lenses to our faces, but with ears and noses to do the job—along with hearing and smelling—it was made simple.

If you were building a person, with no existing model to follow, would you think to cushion the part we sit on? Or install a spine that bends and flexes? Would you pack the operating systems neatly inside a porous-but-waterproof external casing, and line up the parts so they work together or separately as their various functions demand? Without ever having witnessed a skull that covers a brain, would you think to protect the master processing unit inside a hard shell?

We can't answer these questions because we don't know what it's like not to be human with a human point of view. Even if we poke fun at the shape and size of our parts and those of others, our own makeup is something to think about with awe and wonder. Cell upon cell, all add up to this gift in which we live, our bodies.

If that's not amazing, nothing is.

What's humbling is that we did not invent ourselves. We can't take credit for our hands, our eyes, or any other part of us. We can enhance the bits we like and hide the others, but it's hard to do better than a basic model that comes in a unique edition for every single person.

Of course, we aren't the only living things on the planet constructed with attention to form and function. The obviously remarkable creatures are the ones with which we're the least familiar. If you live where I do, these could include elephants, kangaroos, tarantulas, and penguins. We wonder at them, but there are living things close to home that are equally marvellous. Look at the way a bird's wing spreads and flaps, how each feather has a certain place, how many kinds of birds there are. The life cycle of a frog or a butterfly is wondrous, but so is something as simple as the way a frog swims or a butterfly finds flowers. Look at how creatures as diverse as deer and beaver use their tails to signal danger; or how a cumbersome, flub-dubby seal becomes so graceful in water; or how a fish's scales are applied so perfectly to its body. Anyone who has ever watched an ant or a bee colony at work can only marvel at the similarities to our human communities. We admire the blossoms of flowers. We exclaim over leaves and how they grow along stems, some opposite each other and some in whorls and some every which way. We marvel at the way plants and animals protect themselves or hunt for their dinner. And we have to ask ourselves: is this all completely accidental? Could we have created all this ourselves?

WHY?

Today I turned over a chunk of firewood and found a miracle. A tiny, greenish-black salamander with pale green polka dots on its back lay perfectly still on the slimy brown grass. After a moment it stretched and lifted its head, like an infant waking up. I gently moved it to a safer spot, far from my wood-stacking project. Eventually it crawled away.

Finding a salamander could be a "so what?" moment. But consider all the rain that fell in the previous month, the cold nights, and the recent winter, and then consider this tiny naked survivor. While we're sitting in our warm houses staring at pelting rain and listening to the wind howl, these little creatures are outdoors living under rocks and pieces of wood. Unlike humans, salamanders are designed to not only survive, but thrive, in these challenging conditions. That's the miracle of a salamander.

Spring is full of wonders. Dandelions force their way through concrete sidewalks against all odds, nests full of eggs reveal a bunch of hungry open beaks, and new life bursts out all around us. Other seasons bring their own miracles: the uniqueness of a single snowflake, a brilliant sunset, the power of the sea and the wind, the changing leaves. These phenomena inspire awe and wonder, but we don't generally think of them as miracles. We know that someone, somewhere, can explain them away with talk of cells and electrons and other scientific terms.

Unexplained healing is considered to be a miracle, one that twenty-first-century skeptics attribute to science. Not long ago, a physician who found a cure for a life-threaten-ing disease casually commented to reporters that God could take credit for his patients' recoveries. His statement was not news to people who believe in miracles. What made head-lines was not the discovery, but the fact that a man of sci-ence gave credit to God. He had crossed a line, stepped out-side a boundary. It recalled to me a conversation I had with a doctor many years ago about a child's potentially terminal illness. A new, successful treatment had been developed, but no one understood exactly why it worked. "God made it that way," the doctor said. That doctor was at the top of the heap, a recognized expert in that particular illness, and a renowned scientist, but he also accepted that some things are beyond human knowledge.

It surprises us when intelligent, well-educated folks admit they don't know everything. It shouldn't be a shock, because the more we learn, the more we discover how much we don't know. To anyone whose life's work is a quest for knowledge through continuous study and research, the sheer volume of the unknown must be overwhelming. The scope of the world's mysteries is infinite, and it would be arrogant and ignorant to assume that we have all the answers.

My dictionary says that a miracle is an amazing or wonder-ful event that occurs outside the known rules of the universe and is thus caused by divine or supernatural intervention. Once upon a time, earthquakes, eclipses, northern lights, and rainbows were considered to be miraculous signs of God's work. They still wow us, but because a miracle today may be revealed as scientific cause and effect tomorrow, many of us no longer think of these phenomena as divine messages.

It's likely that in the last thirty years science has found an explanation for the cure of the childhood disease mentioned earlier, and that the doctor who spoke of God healing his patients will one day be able to explain it in molecular terms. But do scientific explanations automatically mean these events are no longer miracles? Just because we can explain, for instance, that sunlight shining through moisture at a certain angle creates a rainbow, does that explain the particular spectrum of colours thus created? And if we can explain that, can we explain why? Can we explain ourselves right back to the source? Do our explanations mean there is no longer room for God in the wonderful? Is there a point where we will know absolutely everything and can stop asking to have miracles explained?

Maybe.

But like the salamander, we are designed to be what we are. And being human means that we will continue to ask, "Why?"

MEMBERS OF CREATION

Travel broadens the mind. I discovered the truth of this statement during a trip that took me almost as far from home as possible while still in Canada. Yes, my head feels larger. First my eyes opened wide to encompass the western mountains, plains, rivers, glaciers, the Pacific Ocean, and the multitudes of people in all the big cities and tiny hamlets, the rivers of traffic, dramatic architecture, and the utter vastness and magnificence of it all. The view from my Nova Scotia home is of trees and fields and hills and brooks and beaches and sea, and while it's more than a little beautiful, it's good to be reminded that mine is not the only view in the world.

My ears were opened, too. I was curious to hear what everyone had to say and what they were saying it about. The differences and the similarities among people always amaze me. Whether the folks I met were from large cities like Calgary, San Francisco, or Montreal, or from obscure communities like Old Crow, Keble, and West Bolton, they spoke of the same day-to-day concerns, about survival, being loved and accepted, and having a purpose in life. On the other hand, their individual experiences have shaped their psyches and their souls.

A retired ski jumper talked about seeing as much of the world as he could manage in the time he had left. His wife had died long ago; he was lonely and sought the company of other people. A youngish mother from a mountaintop in Oregon confessed this was her first trip away from home. Her isolation was evident in her preconceived notions about anyone living outside her hometown, but she had a generous and independent spirit and was eager to ask questions.

It took little prodding for a prospector, still hunting a fortune and tight-lipped about his claim on a remote Yukon mountain, to give a bunch of strangers an impromptu and memorable lecture about the gold-seeking process. He spent much of the year grimly alone with his rocks, but he turned out to be wise and entertaining.

A Hollywood film producer talked mostly about his relationship with his grown children. A woman with a hoity-toity accent peered avidly at birds through huge binoculars while complaining about the environmentalists who protested oil drilling. A frustrated federal employee spoke bitterly about the gap between Ottawa's perceptions and those of the people represented by their MPs. A pair of sophisticated globetrotters served us tea in fine bone china and showed off their solar- and wind-powered off-the-grid home.

It all proves that humans are a complicated and exciting mix of opposites and the unexpected. That discovery makes the mind grow, which begs the question: if a mind is not ready for expansion, is it possible for travel, or anything else, to broaden it? We've seen tourists who turn up their noses at whatever they visit and compare it unfavourably to home, wherever that may be. Do they go home with more or *less* understanding of the world? Do their experiences even register a blip on their spirits?

If our minds are grasped in a vise of suspicion and fear, it's hard to expand them, even by travelling to amazing places. Eliminating our suspicion and fear involves exposure to things that unnerve and frighten us. That means getting outside our comfort zones, even if we start by visiting the next street. A trip away, large or small, teaches us that there is something else out there besides our immediate surroundings. It can introduce us to other points of view, and prove that differences are not the same as threats. It can teach us that we are small, humble dots in a huge and powerful creation. Travelling makes us realize that we are not standing on the edge of that creation, watching it, but that we are standing in it. We are members of something awe-inspiring and magnificent, and some of that wonder is reflected in us.

THIN PLACES

In Celtic spirituality or theology, thin places are where people feel acutely closer to the mysterious and awesome power that many of us call God. The division or wall between humanity and the divine is understood to be so thin in these places as to be almost transparent. Spiritually, our connection to the Creator seems so clear and real in thin places that there is a sensation one could reach out and return God's touch.

The notion of thin places has been around since ancient times. Our ancestors, just like us, feared what might be on the other side of the veil between humanity and deity. Would there be blessings or retribution? After crossing over, could one ever return? Thin places can be sites traditionally deemed holy or sacred, such as shrines, churches, or burying grounds. We can choose to visit them in groups or alone. Wherever they are, we expect to feel a divine presence there, a sense of being surrounded by something that's bigger, better, and more important than ourselves. Maybe years of worship in these places make them thin, or maybe they were thin already and that's why people choose to worship there. We don't know.

There are other thin places where individuals may feel kinship to God but which haven't attracted hordes of people, because not everyone has the same experience. Some of us are most sensitive to God's presence on lonely mountaintops or shorelines, in deep woods or barren deserts, on the open sea or high in the air. There are also moments in our lives that could be called thin times. The birth of a baby, overwhelming love, the sudden realization of a mind-blinding truth, and meditation: in these moments our sense of God's presence transcends everything else. That's not to say God gets closer to us in thin places, because God never went away in the first place. These are places where *we* get closer to God.

It seems there are also thin seasons dating back thousands of years. A look at the calendar shows that religious festivals and observances from different faith traditions frequently land on similar dates. People all over the world may be celebrating or worshipping or fasting at the same time. For instance, around December are the Christian Christmas, Jewish Hanukkah, part of the Muslim pilgrimage of Dhū al-Hijjah, the anniversary of the Buddha's enlightenment, and many ancient and neo-pagan solstice observances. Holy days set according to lunar or solar cycles reflect our wonder at changing daylight hours, the many faces of the moon, the tides, and the alignment of the planets. Our awe makes us tingle with the nearness of God, and we feel the presence of holiness. These are thin seasons.

Monuments like Stonehenge were erected according to time rather than place, and reflect a long-standing consciousness that humanity is affected by the positions of the Earth, moon, and sun, along with the other planets and stars. These heavenly objects are places, but their movements and interrelationships create what we understand as time. Earth turns once in twenty-four hours, giving us a day, and the moon takes twenty-eight of those days to circle Earth, giving us a month. We understand time as dependent on the temporary position of a planet or a moon, but how much more is out there, somewhere, that we don't understand at all?

If we can get our heads around the idea that we are part of a great, whirling cosmos where time and place rely on each other, and understand that we are a very small speck in the universe, then we will experience a very thin moment, one when anything is possible. It's a moment when we can believe that God is, indeed, right here with us.

LIGHT AND DARK

Light and dark are strong themes in our spiritual lives, dating back to humanity's earliest days.

Darkness was a time of danger for our distant ancestors, for whom it was just as possible to be eaten as it was to eat. Darkness meant cold as well as fear, and they welcomed the sun's warming rays at dawn, and the increasing daylight of spring. They developed some rituals to mark morning and the solstice and others to protect themselves at the onset of darkness and winter. Some were purely practical, like bringing big logs into their homes to burn during cold weather; others were purely spiritual, like praising their god for another day.

Fast forward to the twenty-first century. The touch of a finger can change dark to light, and back again. There are fewer reasons to be afraid of the dark or to exult in the light, yet light and dark remain powerful cultural and spiritual images. We're in the dark, we snicker pensively at dark humour, we have dark secrets, we see the light, there's a light at the end of the tunnel, and we shed light on a subject.

Religious worship frequently involves lighting candles and fires (or electric lights, as at Christmas), marking prayer times by the angle of the sun, or watching for particular patterns of the stars and planets in the night sky. These acts all recognize the importance of light, but it seems to me that light has different functions in our lives and in our worship and faith traditions. For example: When the Israelites fled from Egypt, they followed a cloud by day and a fire by night;

in the Christian tradition, the wise men from the East followed a star to find the baby Jesus; Saul of Tarsus was blinded by a brilliant light on his way to Damascus to hunt and persecute Christians, whom he saw as a threat. Light from the fiery pillar showed the Israelites the path out of slavery and bondage, so they could make their way to a new land and a new beginning; the light from the star showed the wise men the way, but the destination was confirmed through their years of research and study; Saul's light led him to a new personal belief system and way of life, and a new identity as St. Paul. That light is like the illuminated strip along the airplane floor showing the way to the emergency exits in case of a crash. It's the kind of light you need when you don't know where you're going, when you want guidance and are willing to follow where the light takes you.

But light exposes as well as leads. The Book of Kings tells us how Elijah was taken up to heaven in a glowing, fiery chariot. Elijah's protégé Elisha watched the phenomenon—not something everyone got to see—and the experience marked Elisha's future. Shortly before Jesus's execution, his followers Peter, James, and John saw him, the man they believed was the Messiah, bathed in bright light on a mountaintop while he conversed with long-dead Jewish prophets. It was a once-in-a-lifetime exhibition of supernatural power, and the three disciples were warned not to tell about it, at least not right away. Siddhartha Gautama's experience of hardship and deprivation, a kind of darkness, led him to enlightenment, a deep spiritual understanding that is the foundation of Buddhism. These are the eye-openers, like the light bulb over the heads of comic-book characters when they come to a sudden realization. These experiences don't happen without bravely "shining a light," or examining a situation openly to see truth. Elisha's desire to assume Elijah's ministry, the disciples' faith and deep interest in their Messiah, and Siddhartha's dedication to a life of meditation: all drove them to see things in a better light, both physically and spiritually.

Each of us also has personal light, which may be demonstrated by a glowing face or shining deeds. I like to think of it as the light of solidarity or a love-light, a light that takes a physical presence in candlelit ceremonies or vigils, or a spiritual one in encouraging and helping others to overcome suffering. Some people call it an aura. It's obvious in some folks, and it seems completely absent in others, but I believe it lurks somewhere in each of us.

As important as it is, light would never be visible without darkness. One tiny candle burning in the dark is brighter than several hundred, thousand-foot candles of electric bulbs. A lighthouse shining across a dark ocean symbolizes rescue better than the glow from a busy airport runway. Just as one small kind act in a world of hurt is a beacon for the suffering, and a voice crying in the wilderness is more audible than a boom box at a party, the lights of our spirits shine best in the dark times, when they are needed.

THE UNIVERSE AND BEYOND

It blows me away that Colonel Chris Hadfield sent me photos every day from the International Space Station. I'm not special. Tens of thousands of people from all over the world subscribed to Hadfield's Facebook newsfeed, managed by his son and fed by the Colonel's Twitter account. But the technology still amazes me. In 1991 my family still had a rotary phone and a party line, and like many Canadians I remember crank telephones and asking the operator to dial the number. Plenty of my friends still have dial-up Internet. There is no cable service where I live, and fibre optics aren't even on the horizon. So seeing daily photos from space was quite a leap.

What would my grandfather say about what I can see on my computer monitor? His life spanned the first airplane flight and the first moon landing, which we grandkids watched with him on his little black-and-white television, purchased especially for the occasion. He firmly believed the historic moment was filmed on a Hollywood set and transmitted to the rabbit ears of his. We laughed at his conspiracy theory. Now I know how he felt. Can this be real?

But why not? The space station circles the Earth a mere 330 to 405 kilometres away from us. Think Truro to Fredericton or Ottawa to Toronto: it's not far. We fully expect messages to travel easily and swiftly across those distances over Earth's curved surface. So from the distance angle, it's not such a big deal to receive messages from the space station. But it *is* the angle, or, more accurately, the perspective, that amazes.

Things look different from out there.

Who knew that ocean currents make curly white patterns, or that wind-rippled sand can be seen from four hundred kilometres away? Or that the island of Newfoundland, rumoured to be naught but a rock, gleams like polished silver; or that irrigation projects in Africa appear as abstract swirls of colour? Sure, flying in an airplane one can look down and pick out squares of farmland, the baldness of mountaintops, the velvety folds of foothills, the herring-bone patterns of forestry operations, blue or silver waterways, the roads, the pipelines, the cities, and the towns. But from his seat, Col. Hadfield's physical view of the Earth was that of a round, vivid piece of creation. He couldn't see the evil that divides people and nations, and threatens the planet.

It comes to mind that Hadfield's view was something like God's—except that air and space travel long ago exploded the notion that God is up there or out there, in a separate physical place called heaven. We no longer think of God-in-the-sky, which reinforces the concept that if God is anywhere, (s)he is everywhere. If God is present in the beauty of a Canadian landscape, can God possibly be absent out there, past the clouds, or even past the sun? There is obviously "stuff" in outer space, so how can it not be part of creation? Therefore, how can each of us not be part of creation? If God is present at a birth in Moncton, can God be absent from a similar miracle of life in Talcahuano or Vladisvostok or Timbuktu? If God enfolds the spirit of a dying person here, God must do the same over there—or out there.

Our individual differences are as real and exciting as the contrast between land and water: single exquisite brush strokes on one giant, beautiful canvas that we can't even see. At least, not yet. But human experience predicts that some day our descendants will understand what we can now only imagine today, just as our distant ancestors once believed the sun travelled around the Earth and that lightning signified divine displeasure. In the meantime, we can ask ourselves, if God can be everywhere in the universe, why not in the next life? And we can only imagine what happens after we die. But one day, one way or another, we'll know.

THE TRILLIUM

In the spring there are dozens, maybe hundreds of painted trilliums in the woods near my house. But one spring, a particular trillium stood out. It grew in a patch of earth that had been ploughed, rain-soaked, and then packed hard by machinery. The mud had dried to a cement-like toughness, and not even stubborn blackberries could push through it.

Then this lonely little flower poked its pretty head above the ground.

I have a photo to prove it: the pink and white petals—bracts, for the purists out there—nodding on a slender green stem, with the baked, cracked earth all around. You might expect a rugged dandelion to pop through pavement, but not this frilly, fragile-looking trillium. To me, that little flower represented triumph over adversity, beauty arising from ugliness, hope overcoming desolation.

But why should it be a surprise when circumstances don't predict the outcome? People from difficult beginnings grow into leadership positions, while those born to expectations of greatness may languish in happy obscurity. But not always. A beautiful body can hide an empty mind, and a ravaged and worn exterior may give no hint of internal brilliance, but it's not a hard and fast rule. A red sunset may predict a fine day tomorrow, but don't bet the ranch on it, because the good weather may pass by and dawn may bring rain.

The best team doesn't always win the tournament, and the most qualified person doesn't always get the job. Hard work is not always rewarded, and virtues like honesty sometimes get us in trouble. The janitor may turn out to be displaced royalty, while buddy in the penthouse corner office simply warms a company chair. Either nothing good comes out of Nazareth, or something really wonderful comes out of Nazareth. Life is full of surprises. We can't assume an outcome based on appearances or what we think we know.

So when we expect a patch of bare, hard ground to yield a sturdy dandelion, an extroverted flower that can grow anywhere, we might get a shy trillium instead (or not). My dainty little trillium surprised me by toughing its way into the light, but the lowly and much-maligned dandelion is full of surprises too. You can eat its leaves, make wine or jelly from its blossoms, and make a coffee substitute from its roots. And just have a look at how a dandelion spreads its seeds, by those little fairy parachutes that float around on the wind; meanwhile, trillium seeds are carted around by ants—who knew?

If a tiny flower can move aside a thick canopy of hard-packed mud and butterflies can fly from here to Mexico, what are we humans worried about? As primates with opposable thumbs and a few more brain cells than the average weed or bug, we are quite amazing creatures in our own right. We may not be more important than any other creature, but we appear to be more complex.

So when we get buried in a couple of metres of metaphorical mud, or worry that our lives are unproductive or drab, we can think of the brainless-but-beautiful trillium pushing its way to survival, or the ubiquitous dandelion puffing out little seed umbrellas to populate the world with yellow every spring.

We are part of a wonderful world, as obedient to expectations as any other bit of creation, which means we are full of surprises too.

PART II

God's Gift to Us

LIFE: JUST LONG ENOUGH

How fast things grow, especially when it rains a lot. The grass is barely mowed before it's shaggy again. Hoe the weeds one day, and they're rampant the next. The strawberries blossom and ripen and then overripen. The lettuce is going to seed, and the alder stumps have sprouted hip-high saplings. God's creation is marvellously unfolding, and quickly.

It's possible that things really are growing faster now than in past years. This year's garden was planted a full two weeks earlier than my first, planted at the same spot many years ago. Frost hasn't touched it either, so maybe global climate change is responsible for the rainforest growing outside my door. But that doesn't explain why the robin's eggs in the nest under my deck have already hatched, and the babies have already grown feathers and flown the coop. It seems to have happened so quickly, although by my calendar it took no less time than last year's robins.

And then there are the children. When they are little, they take forever to learn to talk and walk and toilet train. Once they get their first teeth, it's a few years before they need the services of the tooth fairy. Then all of a sudden they have big grown-up smiles. We are so excited for our children on their first day of school, but when we turn around they're graduating. In times of stress we wonder if they're ever going to grow up, and in a blink of an eye they do, and we wonder where our babies went.

Maybe time just disappears into the black hole of the to-do list. The projects, the hobbies, the relationships, the travel, the career, everything that we plan combines to fill more and more hours of more and more days. The great mountain of things we want to do doesn't get done—or at least not all of it—and we keep adding to the pile without subtracting from it. Maybe the sense of time zipping by as we age is a mechanism to remind us that our lives are finite. We become more aware of the fact that someday we will die, and that if we want to achieve our dreams before then we'd better get a wiggle on. That notion energizes those who embrace each day as a new and exciting adventure. Instead of counting the days, they make the days count. For others, the idea that life will end in a year or even thirty is immobilizing. These people decide they've no time left to begin anything new, so they sit and wait. They don't start because they believe they have already finished.

In reality, everyone's day has twenty-four hours, and most of us don't know how many more we have. Compared to the age of the Earth or the universe, we are short-lived creatures, and insignificant. Most of us go through life unnoticed except by our nearest and dearest, and we are, each of us, most important to ourselves. Compared to the robins under my deck or the weeds in my garden, however, we are huge, noisy, fearsome creatures with incredible abilities to inflict change. It's of enormous significance to the robins and weeds if we close off the deck or decide to hoe the garden.

The length of our lives is relative. What we do with the time we have is the issue. After sleeping and other essential habits, the rest is up to us. In the age of self-help books, life trainers, and the Internet, as well as traditional sources of advice like parents, teachers, and religious leaders, there's no shortage of guidance to help us out when we become confused. We can tumble through life like a twig in a torrent, or we can float along on a calm broad river, but usually it's a bit of both. Eventually we all reach the same destination, but it's the quality of our lives, not the quantity, that matters. Quality here doesn't mean a comfortable or even pain-free life. It means using our physical, mental, and spiritual resources in the best way possible, treating others the way we would like to be treated, and keeping our hearts and minds open to new experiences. It involves the form our lives take and the choices we make.

Our lives are God's gift to us. What we make of them is our gift to God. It takes a lifetime, but however long that is, it's just long enough.

SING

A visitor entering our house to the strains of The Rankins' *North Country* should be prepared to eat freshly baked bread and pizza. It's my husband's cooking music, and even if I hear it at the gas pumps I expect to smell bread baking. Our road-trip music has to include Gordie Sampson and CCR, and hearing their tunes anywhere makes me want to search for a map, keys, and sunglasses. I can't wrap Christmas gifts properly unless accompanied by Liona Boyd's classical guitar, and the closing notes of "O Canada" make me want to clap my hands and cheer. If "Smoke on the Water" comes unexpectedly through my car radio, up goes the volume, down go the windows, and bob goes the head: I'm a kid again.

There is music for everything—every situation and every mood. Music can also create moods and set the stage, a fact that marketers and blind dates know well. Elevator music, romantic music, mall music, "on-hold" music—none of it is accidental. Music can make us feel a certain way and make us want to do certain things. How many people, like me, want to start an exercise routine when workout music is played at a dance? Or fall asleep on hearing the last few bars of the evening newscast theme song? (Or the first, depending on one's preference.) Will anyone of a certain age ever forget the shivery suspense engendered by the *da-dum, da-dum* bit of music in the movie *Jaws*? Or the forever-summer feeling brought on by the Beach Boys?

Music's effect on our spirits sometimes takes us by surprise. For some, tears spring unexpectedly upon hearing

"The Lord's My Shepherd" or the Navy hymn because last time they heard it was at a funeral for someone they loved. We can find ourselves grinning like fools all because a melody reminds us of a funny personal experience. Or we can get an inappropriate song stuck in our heads and find ourselves humming "Joy to the World" during a funeral procession. When a snowstorm cancelled Easter church services one year, it didn't feel very holy with all the shovelling and scraping. But when the local radio station's usual Sunday morning broadcast of religious music featured Easter hymns, it became a lot easier to focus on the day's meaning. For me, the soaring voices and triumphant organ music lifted the day from ordinary—quite a feat for what is essentially a series of sounds strung together.

Words, too, are basically sounds strung together as communication symbols for thoughts, but they are taken very seriously for the good or evil they can do. Why should we take music any less seriously? Music coupled with words magnifies its effects. On first hearing a song, we may say to ourselves, "Yes, that's exactly how I feel." Lyrics give us the comfortable knowledge that we are not alone in whatever is going on in our lives at that point. They may make us laugh or cry. They may calm or cheer us, or make us think more deeply about a previously ignored facet of life.

But once we become accustomed to the words, we don't need them to attain that same state of mind. The tune alone hums along our brains' pathways to elicit a response. Through the ages, composers of all genres have known this. National anthems and school or club songs stir our loyalties; slow dirges underscore solemn, mournful occasions; protest songs urge us to action; country music taps into the everyday joys and sorrows we all experience; rock music throbs to the beat of our hearts—or maybe it's the other way around. And on it goes.

Music's effect on the human spirit is not lost on organized religion, which has co-opted some of the best music on the planet. For instance, the lyrics for Leonard Cohen's 1984 release "Hallelujah" have been replaced with words reflecting Christmas and Easter messages. Folks familiar with Scottish poet Robbie Burns's "Ye Banks and Braes o' Bonnie Doon" of 1792 will recognize the tune to the hymn "All Things are Thine" by John Greenleaf Whittier, written almost a century later. Cohen's contemplative music, interspersed with triumphant "hallelujahs," speaks well to the human experience of the cycles of joy and sorrow, while even without the words, the lilt of "Ye Banks and Braes"—originally an ancient dance tune called "A Caledonian Hunt's Delight"—can encourage cheerful Christian charity.

Slow, sad dirges underline the sorrow of Good Friday, Remembrance Day, and funerals; simple plainsong chants in a minor key fit prayerful contemplation; a bit of swing tells a story and shares a message; strong chords make statements of faith or commitment, and loud hallelujahs and soaring Glorias celebrate joy.

Music fits the mood and the message, but only if someone hears it. Music is another gift of the spirit: it must be shared in order to be. So, as nineteenth-century composer Robert Lowry said, "How can I keep from singing?"

ANGELS

A minor crisis in the form of a flat tire stopped me in my tracks on the side of a busy highway, right in the middle of a hot and hectic day. It was my first flat tire in who-knows-how-many years of driving, and I was out of practice in the tire-changing department. But the directions were written on the side of the jack, so no problem.

Unfortunately, only one of the nuts holding the wheel could be budged. Now that is a problem.

Then along came a knight in shining armour.

He was actually an ageless kind of guy, wearing sunglasses and a ball cap and driving a nondescript car so that he could never be recognized again. He was stronger than me. Within ten minutes he had the wheel off and the doughnut on. He analyzed the problem, cautioned me to drive slowly and carefully until the tire was replaced, hopped in his vehicle and disappeared.

That's the kind of person you thank God for. And the nice thing is that the world is full of such angels-to-the-rescue. Not a week goes by that we don't read a thank-you letter in the newspaper from a stranded motorist helped by a stranger, or from the relative of a person taken suddenly ill and cared for by unknown bystanders. Go into a convenience store and find a bottle on the counter to collect change for a sick child's treatment or to help a family made homeless by fire or flood. Check the signs outside fire halls or community centres to see how many benefits are held for citizens in distress or to help disaster-stricken people on the other side of the world. And then there are the legions of quiet helpers, the ones who shovel snow for seniors, or turn up to help with a plugged sink, or give someone a hand stacking firewood, or drop by with a hot meal just when it's needed, or drive people to appointments or the grocery store, or offer to take the kids for the day when child care arrangements fall through.

And they say there are no saints anymore! Hogwash.

It's good to remind ourselves now and again that there really are an awful lot of good people out there. Unfortunately, our attention is so often captured by the evil and trouble in the world that our collective view is of gloom and doom rather than wonder and joy. In the newsgathering business, as in many occupations, watching a steady parade of misery often led me to conclude that the world was going to hell in a basket by the end of next week (or the next week at the latest). And we're still here.

But it's not just the folks regularly scanning society's underbelly who moan about signs of humanity's decay. Every one of us and the family dog rant about the shortfalls of professionals in various walks of life. We decry the younger generation (nothing has changed since I was a member of said generation) for loose morals, strange haircuts, and odd practices. We complain about the stupidity of those who serve the public every day. We *tsk tsk* equally over the callous rich and the shiftless poor. It's true that there are some terribly nasty people in the world—the ones we like to think of as "them." They do awful things, like robbing a motorist stopped with a flat tire rather than changing the wheel. But those folks are few, thankfully.

Compared to the great numbers of mostly good and really good people, the ones we like to think of as "us," or the salt of the earth, the numbers of real nasties are miniscule.

And yes, we all have our moments when we do shameful things. None of us is perfect and we have all done things we rather wish we hadn't. But mostly, we're not so bad. We may not all stop to help a motorist with a flat tire, but it's possible that's because some of us have no idea how to do so. So here's a collective pat on the back to the folks who take the time and energy to do the little things that make a big difference. You make the world a better place.

THE GIFT OF JOY

Amid the most awful experiences, a bird suddenly sings. It may not fit with the universal concept of right and wrong, but time and again the sun shines on a funeral procession, or a tree blooms during tragedy. It was a beautiful day, with much of the world wrapped in joyous Christmas celebrations, when the tsunami struck Southeast Asia with such destructive force in 2004. Exuberant spring was bursting out all over while Westray miners' families waited for word of the men lost underground in the 1992 Plymouth coal mine explosion. And how many times has a child's laughter broken the solemn two minutes of Remembrance Day silence?

It could be offensive, if one was inclined to feel offended. But when we are swamped by grief or pain these little incongruities serve to remind us that life goes on, and that joy exists, somewhere. These tiny moments are comparable to mini-messages from God, too often ignored. We may be too busy wallowing in our own suffering to notice a rainbow or feel the brush of a butterfly's wings, and take them as a sign of better things to come. We want our all-encompassing pain shaken only by an earth-quaking, universe-shattering sign—one we will quite likely interpret to mean more trouble ahead.

When we hope and pray for our miserable situations to change, we should expect that the answer might involve an unpleasant process. We do not get whisked from sorrow to happiness, from poverty to wealth, or from misery to heartiness in the blink of an eye or the wave of a magic wand. Change for the better takes time, effort, and, often, pain.

If we are the authors of our own misfortune, change takes some honest self-examination: not fun, not magic, and not pretty. If we are the victims of someone else's evil ways, change may take the form of courageous resistance or brave action: not fun, not magic, and not pretty.

Recovering from serious illness involves injections, surgery, and other painful and uncomfortable procedures. Getting over the death or departure of a loved one involves a process of grief that we may deny at our peril. Acquiring an education involves studying, homework, and the sacrifice of time and resources. Changing a drab backyard into a beautiful garden means muddy, broken fingernails and a sore back—or a depleted wallet if someone else is paid to do it.

With violent change, the resultant misery and suffering is obvious, and begets even more prayer to end the death and suffering. When the symptom of change is pain for gain, no wonder we humans might prefer patience. But sometimes change is the only option, even if we have to shoulder the burden alone.

In the deepest, darkest part of those struggles, a bird singing, a flower opening, or the clutch of a baby's hand can give us a feeling of hope and joy that is sometimes frightening in its intensity. As strange as joy may feel in the midst of suffering, we should maximize every joyful millisecond, because we can't capture these moments and hoard them. Joy has no price, and can't be bought or stolen.

Wealthy people with multiple homes, cars, boats, vacations, and wardrobes are plagued with as much depression, addiction, and other joyless problems as anyone else. Joy is not identical to relaxation, laughter, satisfaction, or success. It's not something that comes from a bottle or a pill, but from somewhere inside us. We experience joy or happiness in spite of life's problems, not as a result of having none.

The Creator gives us the capacity and ample opportunity to experience joy, but it's our choice to accept and use that gift. We never know what's around life's next corner, but if it is joy we should embrace it. It can be fleeting enough.

HOLY DAYS

A nineteenth-century Halifax businessman once complained about the noise made in a nearby church on Sundays. Like his Lord God, the man worked six days and rested the seventh, and the music disrupted his day of rest. He claimed to follow the fourth commandment, to keep the Sabbath holy, while this noisy church made a mockery of holiness. The music was sacred to that particular religious group, but it annoyed him. He wanted the mayor to fix the situation.

I wonder what the mayor said. Did he tell the businessman to sing his own songs louder to drown out the offending tunes? Did he tell him it was a free country and to live and let live? Maybe he told him that council had no place in the sanctuaries of the town or sent a policeman the next Sunday to turn down the volume. Perhaps he suggested the man stuff cotton in his ears. Or maybe the mayor said nothing.

Canada's 1906 Lord's Day Act, which prohibited businesses from opening on Sundays, began to fall apart almost immediately after being enacted. In order that the country didn't come to a grinding halt on Sundays, essential services like hospitals and police stations were legislated to remain open. Over time, more and more services were deemed "essential." In the 1970s and '80s churches complained about children missing Sunday school and their parents skipping church to attend sports practices and tournaments. In the 2000s Nova Scotia's provincial government lifted the century-old prohibition against Sunday shopping, meaning store employees no longer had the day off to attend church (or to sleep until noon).

It's about money.

There may only be so much of it to go around, but few businesses want to risk losing a day's worth of income by staying closed while another remains open. And few employees shun a Sunday workday, because they fear for their positions and wages. Churches, ostensibly in the business of saving souls and sharing a religious message, don't want to risk holding worship services on a different day of the week or in a different space. Churches want people to have Sundays off with nothing else to do but go to church—and make a monetary offering.

The Creator proved to be the author of common sense by ordering a rest day, which we would keep holy in order to exult in our relationships with God and with each other. We need one day in seven to rest, at a minimum. When we don't have it, we suffer physically, emotionally, and spiritually.

It matters little which of those seven days we choose as Sabbath, but on that day we should pause, put up our feet. The world will not end if we don't do the housework, miss the big sale at the mall, or if the oil sits in the car another day. On that day, we can close our eyes and think about nothing. Before our thoughts and worries return to crowd our minds, we can think about lightness, goodness, and peace. It may require focus, but physical exhaustion can leave us no option but to give up and rest. It feels tremendous, and it is not an illusion. It is more real than all the trappings of holy days— the food, decorations, music, and all the traditions intended to make The Day right.

Christmas is an especially hectic holy day on which to find rest, because we work to meet our own mountainous expectations. We like to pretend that there is no nastiness or fear in the world. We like to believe in a perfect morning, perfect gifts, perfect family gatherings, and a perfect meal. These do not exist outside our imaginations. As imperfect humans, we can't create something perfect or force perfection on someone else. The only person we can move towards perfection is ourselves. Demanding that others cede to our visions of a perfect Christmas violates the season as a celebration of God's gift of ultimate love for us imperfect humans. Despite our dedication to perfection, experience tells us the choir will creak, the power will go out, the turkey will burn, Uncle Whosit will drink too much and Aunt So-and-So will make critical comments, the kids will get tired and weepy, the tree will fall over, and someone will make it plain that an electronic gizmo would have made a much better gift.

We cannot create a perfect Christmas or any other holy day, so it's time to accept our powerlessness and get over it. A holy day is God's gift to us, and our role is to simply and fully experience it. We do it without demanding others to be just like us, which is truly the beauty of love, after all. On our Sabbath day, we should let go of our demanding selves and just be.

STRAWBERRIES

One of my favourite mid-summer activities is the annual trip to the strawberry U-pick. It always happens in July, on a date that depends mostly on the weather. After hosing spiderwebs from the dozens of wooden quart boxes collected in thirty-plus years of berry picking and then jamming them into my seasoned-strawberry-field-veteran's wooden crate, anyone within listening distance is shanghaied to the berry field.

When our house was full of kids, strawberry picking was a way of providing a steady supply of fruit for winter, equal to four or five flats of berries. They had to be rinsed, hulled, and packed away—several hours of work that left our fingernail beds raw and hands stained red. These days we get by with fewer berries, but the summer pilgrimage continues. As the baskets fill, our memories are shared. Now with a third generation of berry pickers, more memories are added to the collection that includes the baby who quietly filled her little face with berries when everyone thought she was asleep in her carrier; the toddler who painted his clothing and everyone else's with berry juice; the unheeded warnings not to eat the berries until we got them home and washed them; the teens who earned college money by working in the berry field; and the day the sky turned green and a mini-tornado blew through while we hulled berries on our back step.

Not much changes from year to year in the strawberry field. The *zzzzst-zzzzst* of busy insects, rows and rows of pickers bent over their task, the sun shining hotly, the lazy conversation about the beauty of the fruit and world affairs, birdsong, the smell of fresh strawberries in the sun, the straw under your knees as you crawl up the rows, and the berry-laden trudge back to the car trying not to trip and lose it all—amazingly, little of it has changed in a world where the only constant is change.

They don't play elevator music at *my* berry field, and the main road is far enough away that the sound of traffic is muted. It's a peaceful place. As an oasis in a troubled world, the berry field holds a strong position. Made captive by the task at hand, one can carry on a conversation with fellow pickers, or just ponder whatever comes to mind. Harvesting fruit—or anything else—is a useful activity, so there's no sense that one is wasting time by enjoying the company of others while working. For those of us who are workaholics, a stint in the berry field can satisfy both the need for productivity and the yearning for personal peace. The stated goal of berry picking is filling the baskets, but so much more is accomplished.

They say you're never as close to God as you are in a garden (or a berry field) but it doesn't have to be so. Many of us find the same connection with the Creator while on a journey. The business of getting from one place to another, by whatever means, can be a solitary task made holy (and whole) by mental activity or in the companionship of fellow travellers. We finally have the chance to read, chat with family members, look out the window or gaze at the clouds, think our problems through, and sometimes come to important decisions. We do this while accomplishing the stated goal of getting from Point A to Point B.

Not everyone can travel or pick fruit, but we all have access to useful tasks that allow us to recreate ourselves, and our souls. Some people fish, but the act of catching food for the table—a useful goal—is often secondary to the act of standing by the water and casting a line. Angling is not really play, but it doesn't feel like work, either. Some people find the same peace when they clean, or bake, or mow, or paint, or iron. The little things we do are as important for our psyches as the big things. If we are able to achieve a sense of joy and peace along with our goals, then our baskets are truly full.

GOD'S GOOD MIRTH

Along a country road near here, I once glimpsed a sign tucked into the trees at the end of a driveway. It said something about how a life can be wonderful if it's spent making people laugh. Or maybe it said that life is not wasted when it is used to make other people joyful, or happy. That was the gist of the message—a squirrel dashed in front of my car just then and diverted my attention. The concept that a life is well spent in comforting others is not a new one, and I forgot about the sign within minutes. But it came back to me later that day, over and over, as I wrote an investigative news account of a young man's death in a car crash.

Reporting on sudden death was a job I had learned to hate. It involved trying to track down enough information about the victim and the circumstances of his or her death in order to give an accurate account that would quell gossip, be sensitive to the feelings of the deceased person's family and friends, and mark with dignity the passing of a community member. The task means being accused of callous nosiness for seeking information, and callous indifference for not including enough of it. It's a bit like walking a tightrope. In the aftermath of this young man's death, however, I was soon reminded of the words on the sign nestled in the trees. Neighbours, friends, and acquaintances all spoke of his ability to lift people's spirits when they were down, his ready smile, and his generous sense of humour.

Not much better can be said about someone than "he/she made the world a better place simply by being in it." Most of us fill that role for the people who love us best, but how many of us can have it said that we can brighten a room simply by entering it? Or that we can bring cheer to total strangers of all ages and walks of life by exercising our own good humour? We often assume people with that ability have happy, easygoing lives with none of the challenges faced by the rest of us. That assumption may give us an excuse not to follow suit, but it may also be wrong.

Smiles and laughter can hide a sad heart and a difficult life as much as they advertise happiness. People with deep sadness in their lives learn quickly that they don't want to be pitied, nor do they want to wallow in their misery. They have learned, as the poet Ella Wheeler Wilcox said, "Laugh and the world laughs with you, weep and you weep alone." The same poem goes on to conclude that pain and sorrow make a narrow path, with little room for a companion to walk with us. A life can be as pain-filled as anyone can possibly imagine, but a cheerful face means one won't be alone. People gravitate towards those who smile.

It's interesting to note that the world's various religions talk about finding joy in the discovery of God's presence, the soul-filling, all-encompassing joy that doesn't simply mask sorrow but pushes it out of the way. So here's a question: do we discover joy in God's presence, or do we discover God's presence in our joy?

I would suggest it's both.

Experiencing God makes us joyous because in joy's purest form all cares slip away, all conflicts cease, hate disappears, and we are at one and in love with the universe. A tall order for sure. Pure joy is a bit harder to find than ordinary, everyday mirth, but laughter can steer us to joy, which can bring us closer to God. Laughter opens us to new people, ideas, and

experiences. (Even a smile changes how our voices sound—
for proof, try it during a telephone call.) That openness lets
joy fall in. Anyone who has ever laughed hard with loved
ones has likely experienced the sudden realization of a joy-
filled moment, a moment when sorrow and pain disappear. It
can start with a joke or someone playing the fool and result
in the joyous recognition that one is surrounded by love.

So, if God *is* love, and shared laughter can lead us to joy
and the experience of love, then being able to make people
laugh can be seen as the ability to prepare people for the
divine. That's quite a gift.

It's also one that's occasionally hard to accept.

True story: A minister presided over a funeral for a person whose family did not belong to any particular church
but who wanted a religious ceremony. The family was, to
paraphrase the minister's description, excessively ordinary,
straight-speaking smokers and drinkers, of mediocre health
and wealth. A fresh, wet snowfall was ankle-deep by the
time the family gathered with the minister at the graveside
for their relative's burial. As soon as the last "Amen" was
uttered, a child pitched a snowball at an adult and within
moments the whole family was in the middle of a snowball fight, shrieking with laughter among the headstones. "I
loved it," the minister told me. "You don't see that kind of
joy in regular church people."

So do "regular church people" take themselves too seriously, or are they scared to feel joy? Indeed, why should I
selfishly mourn the loss of a family member, or feel sorrow
when a loved one has passed into God's joyous presence? It
defies the logic of having faith in an afterlife. I may grieve
the end of companionship upon the death of a loved one, but
if I truly believe that they go to a better place after they die

and I truly love them, then I should feel happiness on their behalf. I may also feel sorrow and guilt for the bad choices I have made, but to punish myself over and over is to ignore God's love and forgiveness.

The refusal to experience joy because we feel we ought to demonstrate sadness to the world shows that we are more concerned about what people think than about what we believe. We exhibit not faith, but fear and uncertainty. Why should our spiritual lives be devoid of laughter, deserted by happiness and joy?

Anyone who attends worship needs only to look around to see mouths drawn down on closed faces. What's that all about? If we are meant to be joyful in God's presence, does this mean God is missing from worship? A scary thought. Why should we take our spiritual lives and ourselves so seriously? Apparently we are the only creatures on Earth that can laugh—and that alone should tell us that we are designed for humour. In the meantime, thank God for the lives that lead us to laughter.

SEASONS

The nice thing about having seasons is that they come just in time. Just as weeding, heat, and frenetic summer activities get tiring, it's autumn: my favourite season. I love the brilliant colours of pumpkins, apples, and cranberries; impossibly blue skies; dramatic clouds; the landscape's last green gasp before the trees pop their autumn glory; clear, crisp weather; extra blankets on the bed; a fire in the wood stove, and, best of all, the rewards of the harvest. It's a time to settle down, to take stock of our material and spiritual blessings. Thus the brilliant month of October ends with that in-your-face attention to death and the hereafter: Halloween.

If any of the macabre trappings of Halloween were real we'd be scared silly, but we revel in creepy costumes, groans, shrieks, lawn cemeteries, glow-in-the-dark bones, and dead-finger cookies. Halloween is an outlet for our fear of death. We all know we're going to die, but we're not spiritually ready, so we're scared. Since ancient days, fall's lengthening darkness has seemed an appropriate season for the dead to visit. Co-opted by Christians as All Saints Day, November 1st became a commemoration of departed souls. The day before, All Hallows Eve, became Halloween, when the knowledge that we'll join the dead nibbles at the psyche of even the least religious person: like the season, we, too, will pass.

After Halloween, when the leaves lie crumpled and dead on the ground and the short grey days grow dreary, snow arrives with its newness and peace, and brings Christmas and other religious festivals, time with family, and winter sports. After shovelling five or six blizzards' worth of snow, winter wears a little thin; suddenly the snow melts, the sap runs, the trees bud, the robins show up, and spring has sprung. About the time the blackflies get too hungry and the mud begins to overwhelm, spring oozes gently into summer. And then it starts all over again.

The motion of the earth around the sun gives us four official seasons, but an old Canadian joke claims we have three months of winter and nine months of hard sledding—a sentiment that defines seasons by something other than the planet's position in relation to the sun. Aboriginal peoples all over the world traditionally reckon seasons by the cycles of nature, while sports enthusiasts count time by the coming and going of hockey or baseball season. We have silly season, income tax season, tourist season, back-to-school season, blackfly season, planting season, hunting season, fishing season, ski season, construction season.… We assign a season for everything, and everything a season. It's an old concept.

Back in the early '60s, folk singer Pete Seeger recorded a song about the seasons of life, almost entirely cribbed from a much older passage attributed to King Solomon (Book of Ecclesiastes, chapter 3). The song goes, in part: "To everything…there is a season…and a time to every purpose under heaven": a time to be born, a time to die, a time to plant, and a time to pluck up what was planted. Seeger used these words to plead for world peace. The same words may also be used as an excuse to kill or mouth off, but they are more observation than permission. They report the obvious: When the soil and weather are right and there is time to grow crops, then it's time to plant. When something saddening happens, it's time to mourn. We buy snow tires when winter's coming, and we stock up on finger foods for Stanley Cup season. We react to and prepare for the situations and seasons as they cycle past. And they do pass.

Even in the midst of difficult seasons and the most wonderful events, we know that they will pass. So we experience the good with joy, and suffer the difficult with hope. Because things will change.

PLANET EARTH

In 2003 a sneeze in China caused an epidemic in Toronto. The following year a tsunami in Indonesia caused ripples at beaches around the world. Both events demonstrate the world's connectivity. Just as we humans are made up of our souls and minds and bodies, so is the Earth made up of interdependent facets: humanity, geography, flora, fauna, and even the atmosphere that cushions us from space. Events in one place can drastically affect people or animals or mountains in another.

Humans have the ability to create great change, but what of our responsibility for that change? Unlike rivers, oceans, plants, and animals, we humans mostly choose our actions. Do we want their effects to be positive or negative? In 2007 Acadia University biologist Dr. Donald G. Dodds wrote an essay called "A Good-bye Hope," in which he urged everyone to treat God's Earth with love. His essay begged us to stop seeing the Earth as a personal store full of goodies, somehow magically replenished for every succeeding generation. Instead, he urged us to see it as a precious gift shared with all life—not only now, but in the future. Dodds, who died in 2010, made it clear that humanity belongs to the Earth and is part of its great cycle of life, not separate from it; that we must treat each other and the whole world as creations of God, knowing that all living things have a place in the universe.

We shouldn't have to be told that when coal is burned up, it's gone, or that when water is polluted, it's expensive and time-consuming to clean. When all the fish are dead, they can't make more—ghosts don't procreate. It's not necessary to our survival or even our comfort to eat all the Earth's fish, trash the rivers and seas, or use the planet's entire fuel supply. We devour abundantly because we can. Even the term "natural resources" symbolizes a mindset that sees the Earth as existing solely for human consumption, until it's all gone. According to this self-centred view, the Earth and its bounty exist solely for those who are powerful enough to seize it. Thus, we grant ourselves permission to kill, steal, enslave, and destroy in order to achieve personal wealth. Once we move past the struggle to simply survive, we are driven to achieve. We bask in our success and ignore its effect on the world around us, and on the future. We disregard the cruelty of robbing our children and grandchildren for the sake of present indulgence.

It is frustrating to conscientiously sort recyclables, reuse and repurpose, drive fuel-efficient vehicles, or heat with solar, only to watch someone else gobble the tiny bit of planet we just rescued. It is disheartening to repeat warnings against fouling our nests, our neighbourhoods, and our Earth, only to realize that no one listens. But lessons repeated and practiced are lessons learned—and, hopefully, passed to future generations. For our own survival and that of our children and grandchildren, we must learn to love, protect, and nourish our own little corners. That includes the people, animals, plants, air, water, and even the dirt.

Our care for our world must stand in awe of the magnificence of Creation because, in spite of our technological advancement, we have not been able to mirror it. Nor are we able to reverse our grave errors. Three hundred years after humans exterminated the dodo bird, it remains extinct, and our stubborn dependence on fossil fuels has caused pollution of land, water, and air—not to mention global climate change. We are incapable of turning back the clock on our poor stewardship of the Earth. We are trashing our only home, God's gift to us, and we need to stop.

PART III

The Trouble with Us

SMUG AND SECURE

Some days are just bad days. Oversleep, run out of coffee filters, there's no hot water, the car won't start, traffic is heavy, the boss is in a filthy mood, and half the office is out with an illness that seems to strike everyone else before day's end. The drive home is slowed by miserable weather and traffic, and there's an unexpected bill in the mailbox. The front-door key is temporarily misplaced and everything lands on the doorstep during the search for it, breaking whatever is breakable. Open the door and the power is off, a pet has made a mess of whatever, there is nothing to eat, the phone rings with disturbing news about mutual funds, and the landlord drops in with a notice about a rent increase. On top of all that, the bed is in exactly the same mess it was when it was left in the morning.

But then the power comes on, and so does the TV. And there, right in the living room, is an earthquake victim. He's screaming that his family is buried underneath the rubble. Someone has covered his eyes with what looks like a sock, because he hasn't seen daylight in a week and the light hurts—along with God knows what else. As they carry him away on a stretcher, a pleasant but sombre voice announces that anyone found after today will likely be dead, buried alive in a landslide or under a collapsing building.

Change the channels, rummage in the cupboard for a can of soup and some crackers. Perch on the edge of the couch with a bowl and a plate to see, across the room and as large as life, a man carrying a scrawny, big-eyed, scantily clad child.

The child has his arms clamped around the man's neck as they wade through a flooded street, following a line of others also plodding through the rain. They pay no attention to the camera, which pulls back for a different angle, showing a row of flimsy houses tipping dangerously into the water. The camera pans across an anxious-looking woman clutching an infant. Another pleasant but sombre voice announces that foreign aid can't get through to these people. Thank you, the news anchor says to the correspondent reporting from the rain and muck, before turning to show folks in living rooms a different background.

On the other side of the coffee table appear the dust and the *pop-pop-pop* of guns on a deserted street in a battered country on the other side of the world. There's a groan, and someone falls in front of the camera. Suddenly there appears what looks like a camp cot, but that ubiquitous pleasant but sombre voice says it's a hospital bed. The child in the cot is moaning weakly, and a woman strokes the kid's bandaged head as she looks hopefully up at someone who might be a doctor, a nurse, or someone who can help. The voice says words like "civilian casualties" and "collateral damage."

Wander to the desk with one eye on the television, take out a chequebook, and write out payment for that unexpected bill from the mailbox. Look up in time for a commercial break. A once-well-known actress from a long-ago show sits on a rock in front of a dilapidated shanty built of flattened oil cans. A thin, serious-faced child leans against her and another sits on her knee, staring directly, accusingly into the living room. The actress explains that both kids are orphans and have never attended school. They are wearing the only clothes they own, they play with a rock and a rusty tin can, and are lucky to eat once a day. Not only that, there are hundreds of kids just like them in this particular village and in hundreds of other villages. Plaintively the actress beseeches, can't somebody help just one?

Why not? The chequebook is in hand. Fix it up for one hungry, homeless, under-educated orphan. But what about the other victims in the living room—of the earthquake, the flood, and the war? Not far outside the living room, what about the other victims closer to home: the addicts, the suicidal, the sick, the hungry, and the lonely? Well, just turn off the TV and forget them all. Avoid newspapers and magazines and radio. Stay out of the coffee shops. Stay off the streets. Then maybe we can believe it when we tell ourselves we're having a bad day.

Or we could help, even just once.

DOES ANYONE CARE?

Research says that country folk are less healthy than city folk, and apparently the rural folk are at fault. It's a lifestyle thing. Country people eat too much, smoke too much, and drink too much. They visit their physicians too seldom, and when they do make an appointment they are already sick. They move too little, and when they do, they have accidents that maim or kill them. They suffer from depression and loneliness and poverty, and all their attendant ills. But blaming rural residents for a decline in their health is like blaming starving people for showing their ribs. You can't blame people for their poor health when everything in the community that once kept them hale and hearty is taken away.

As rural communities are stripped of everything that made them what they are—or were—those who live there are stripped of their identities as well. With the closure of railway stations, post offices, schools, hospitals, and clinics, mills, banks, retail stores, farms, and gas stations, once-bustling villages have become picturesque hamlets for tourists to view out the window on their way to manufactured attractions somewhere else. Motorists zoom through these places well above the posted speed limit, or bypass the deplorable country roads on a remote four-lane blacktop, and wonder if anyone at all lives in rural Canada.

Most of the people remaining in rural communities are too elderly, poor, or overburdened with family responsibilities to leave. Add to that the stubborn few who see a glimmer of hope in their villages' futures, and the newcomers who want to try rural life until they discover they have to drive at least twenty kilometres in any direction on bad roads to access the services they consider "normal." In the country, one can no longer exercise by walking, or riding bicycles or horses to the store. Whatever the destination, it was likely closed and torn down five years ago, and the trip would mean competing with thundering eighteen-wheelers and RVs for the few good yards of narrow roadway.

It's bad enough when the government and capitalists desert rural communities citing low population levels—what they mean is, there are not enough voters and spenders to make it worthwhile to invest in those places. But when the church turns its back on rural Christians, it's enough to give anyone's health a turn for the worse. More and more of our pretty (usually) clapboard churches of various denominations are being abandoned as congregations find themselves getting too old and decrepit to even ring the bells on Sunday mornings. Rural congregations ride a slippery slope towards closure: Sunday schools empty, teens go off to university and stay away, the choir gets greyer and quavers more on the high notes, the stalwarts move into nursing homes in larger communities, and congregations consolidate so their ministers' attentions are thinly spread among more and more far-flung communities.

Thriving urban congregations frequently have access to accomplished and experienced clergy, or promising new ones—as well as paid janitors, secretaries, and other staff. Sagging rural churches, on the other hand, may get whatever minister can briefly put up with a brutal schedule, life in a fishbowl, precious little earthly reward, and dealing with the non-availability of already overworked volunteers for every little task. Rural congregations everywhere beat their heads against the reality of aging church members and increasing operating costs. They expend their energies just keeping the peeling shingles on the roof and the electricity turned on, leaving little for their real purpose of spreading God's message and doing God's work. And sadly, they get little sympathy or help from their wealthier urban cousins or from their particular denomination's headquarters, far off in a city somewhere.

It's not as if God isn't needed in rural areas. The health concerns alone should be enough to prompt church leaders to stick their long noses into the situation. There are also single parents struggling to teach their children the difference between right and wrong, lonely elders who would cherish a visit and someone to pray with them, teens struggling to discern their futures, middle-aged people putting aside their own long-held dreams to care for aging parents or help misguided offspring, and a host of other miseries—and rural people handle them in isolation. They need the spiritual guidance that can't come from government programs or retail therapy. But the local church has worn itself threadbare, and the greater church organization that administers it is absent.

If anyone at all cares about the future of Christianity outside urban centres, or that of any other religion, policies and attitudes towards country congregations must change.

But maybe no one cares.

OUT OF TOUCH

"Even a king depends on the harvest," says Ecclesiastes 5:9. This short sentence popped up during a search for something else, in the usual way the Book of Ecclesiastes comes to my attention. This three thousand-year-old collection of backcountry wisdom and cynical observation is easily lost. It's just twelve brief chapters of pithy remarks about the nature of God and life, buried about halfway through the Hebrew scriptures.

This particular quotation is tucked away in a rant about oppressive governments and the useless accumulation of wealth, both popular topics today. Substitute the words "government," "prime minister," "president," or "dictator" for the word "king" and rearrange gender pronouns as necessary, and the statement is as true today as it was in Solomon's time. At its most basic interpretation, even a king has to eat. With the exception of photo opportunities, the ruling class is rarely found in fields, barns, or even kitchens, so in order to eat they depend on the harvest and the people who sow, reap, hunt, and gather food and materials.

Kings who snap whips over their people's backs to force a harvest wonder why their empires fail, sometimes within a single generation. It's a no-brainer: if you don't take care of your car, it won't work for you and you won't get anywhere. If you don't take care of your land or your people, the same logic applies. Lucky for the king, if he can't get dinner from the farm down the road, his wealth can buy the harvest of another nation. But he's still only as wealthy as his nation's industry, which, if not based on land and sea, is based on people, who all need to eat.

Few people grow enough food at home to feed themselves, let alone the king. But a king needs something to be king of, so he must ensure his people have adequate food, shelter, and clothing. He must ensure a harvest, somewhere. The loyal subjects aren't stupid. Should a king begin to think he is somehow immune to his nation's dependency on the harvest, that he can ignore the care of the earth and the people who do the nitty-gritty work of caring for it on his behalf, he invites distrust, hatred, ridicule, and rebellion. And once the harvest goes, so goes the king.

This essay could be a rant against the rape of land and sea, a plea to buy locally grown food or for us to treat others as we want to be treated. But the verse from Ecclesiastes is mostly a reminder to those who are detached by circumstance from the land and sea: we all depend on the harvest. If we live in glass and steel towers that loom far above forty hectares of pavement with barely a patch of God's good earth in sight, we depend on the harvest. If we never get dirt under our nails scratching at weeds, shovel a single scoop of manure, haul in a single fish, lift a package of seed, or blister our hands and feet and wear out our backs, we depend on the harvest. The earth matters, because it produces the harvest for us all. Age, time, place, race, gender, wealth, or creed: our survival depends on the harvest. That means all of us, including the king.

SPIRITUAL HEALTH

Is faith more authentic when it kneels publicly to weep with religious passion, or when it prays privately and quietly in a darkened room? Only the Almighty knows. But some people feel uncomfortable with one way, which, they believe, makes their own method correct.

Some religious cultures expect adherents to make a noise, to celebrate loudly, mourn visibly, and exhort with conviction. Others appreciate a more restrained response, with designated places and times for religious activities, maintaining placid facades in between. One faith may shout religious slogans to announce itself, while another may do so through clothing or jewellery, hand signals or body positions, such as kneeling or prostration. The various ways of expressing faith may explain why there are so many religious groups, but it's a chicken-and-egg situation: maybe the existence of so many religious groups resulted in a variety of religious expression.

We've all found ways to express our deepest spirits safely, because if we let them out of the box there is no telling what might happen. Prayer and praise, our approach to God, the mystical work of the Creator in our midst: these experiences have the frightening power to move us to tears, to deep thought, to self-examination and, often, to change. Strong responses are hard to handle day in and day out, and these are just the spiritual confrontations. (It's never happened to me, but a physical face-to-face with my Maker would render me absolutely speechless with awe and completely unable to function physically.) So we set our souls on autopilot while we attend to practical matters like food and shelter. But we can't set our spirits aside for long. They are part of us, just like our minds and bodies—despite science pooh-poohing over the past century the notion that our spirits have any real connection to our minds and bodies. (Apparently, our spirits are our imaginary friends.)

Today, whole industries exist to teach us how to connect mind, body, and spirit. Need proof? Just Google it. Physicians use spiritual exercises to battle cancer and other diseases, while fitness instructors and educators prescribe meditation to overcome physical and mental obstacles. Currently, organized religion is about the only segment in society that isn't fervently advocating a mind–body–soul meld. It's weird, because long-established religions have a solid history of preaching and teaching how the mind, body, and soul intertwine. Unfortunately, religious circles take it for granted that followers already understand this interrelationship. If this assumption were accurate, how would we explain those people who find spiritual sustenance in gyms, clinics, and clubs?

Organized religion tends to package faith and spirituality in a dull-looking box, hide it in a building, and then dare people to come and get it—but only on certain days at certain times. It's rarely delivered (almost never to newbies), and it seldom tumbles into the street or the neighbourhood. That's too bad, because our spirits thrive when nourished in the presence of others. Studying and practising a lively, authentic, and open faith excites our bodies, minds, and souls. It stretches our spiritual experience to new boundaries, and colours our lives with joy.

Spirit can be a powerful, world-altering force that we ignore at our peril. However we display it, publicly or privately, is okay. The Almighty understands.

THE CHRISTMAS CHALLENGE

Every year, campaigns to get rid of Christmas fakery pick up steam. The Advent Conspiracy is one international movement aimed at restoring Jesus's life and teachings as the season's focus. Another, The Buy-Nothing Christmas, is a project by the Canadian Mennonites aimed at de-commercializing Christmas and persuading citizens to give and receive wisely, and with love. Meanwhile, giant chain stores offer to make donations to charity if we buy three of an item—as if they couldn't make donations in any other way. Charities urge us to give to the needy as well as, or instead of, our Secret Santa, office friends, or that great-aunt who already has everything.

Personally, I'd like to reduce the pile of plastic that changes hands every December 25, halt the hype that aims to improve the economy rather than increase spirituality, and put Christ back in Christmas, as the saying goes. My favourite image of Christmas is the hushed expectation of a filled church, followed by voices in joyful praise. The anticipation follows us home, where we enjoy messages from family and friends, sleep in cozy beds while snow lands silently outside the windows, and awake to the bliss of watching children's eyes light as something special emerges from the wrappings.

But I'm all grown up now. I know that image can't be realized without stress. Musicians, singers, and pageant participants fit practice into their busy schedules; clergy prepare memorable sermons about a much-preached-upon subject; and someone has to remember to turn up the heat in the church. There is shopping, crafting, wrapping, penning notes and labels, decorating, cooking and cleaning, sorting out kids who are wound up like cheap clocks, keeping the cat off the tree, and on it goes. Christmas does not land like magic. It is work, and stress—whether we indulge in the commercial frenzy of Christmas-buying and Boxing Day-returning, if we focus purely on the manifestation of God in human form, or on some middle road.

If quitting it all were the Christmas message, why would God have bothered becoming human in the first place? God has the power to pluck us from our misery and store us in capsules to contemplate the Deity forever without distraction, but he doesn't. We are designed to be part of this fussy, mussy world. To withdraw from holiday pressures is a personal choice we can make, a decision itself fraught with stress and angst. We can also choose simply not to give and receive gifts at Christmas, which can be stressful if our loved ones see things differently.

We can choose to give the same gift to each person, no favourites. It's easier than agonizing over every perfect individual demonstration of love, but we may feel a sense of failure when eyes don't alight with joy upon opening a pair of socks. We can choose to bestow our resources on the hungry and homeless, and to feel betrayed or resigned when we discover that most of the funds pay for advertising or staff instead of food or shelter.

Christmas offers opportunities to feel betrayed, tricked, or disappointed—just like life. But it also allows us to bask in the love of family and friends, greet a stranger with unembarrassed joy, talk about our faith, mend broken fences, or reach out to lonely and forgotten people.

We can do that any time, of course. But it's easier at Christmas.

WAR IN GOD'S NAME

Is it possible to wage a religious war?

It would depend on the religion. If our religious affiliation demands that we eliminate everyone who doesn't believe what we believe, destroy all their homes, businesses, schools, and places of worship, all in the name of God, then that conflict would, technically, have a religious purpose. A religion with that goal would worship a god that prefers people dead rather than converted, a circumstance that would result in fewer and fewer followers of that particular deity. And a religion with no members or worshippers defies the logic of its existence.

Followers of that kind of deity and religion would not experience many more benefits than its opponents. Imagine always having to go to war to kill off non-believers, and getting yourself killed in the process (albeit in a noble fashion). Or, after all opposing faiths were eliminated, you'd be looking over your shoulder for the death penalty to follow you for some mistake. Sooner or later everyone would make mistakes and fall afoul of that religion, because it's just not humanly possible to always be right.

What's the point of being God if you plan to rid the planet of your followers?

Why would anyone follow a god that sounds more like a petty human dictator than a benevolent ruler of the universe?

Let's suppose for a moment that God is not like that. Just suppose God loves every single being on the planet—and even those off the planet, should there be any. Just suppose

God even loves the people we don't. Suppose God's greatest wish is that we love each other as much as we love ourselves, and that we love God as much as God loves us. It would make it hard to justify hurting or killing each other in his name. Now suppose some people think God wants all people to live in peace with each other, while others think God prefers the execution of non-believers. All the people who truly believe in a peaceful, loving God act peacefully and lovingly, while the other bunch kills them all off. That leaves only the followers of a warlike religion—who, as described above, would eventually self-destruct. That leaves no religion, which makes it pretty hard to argue in favour of fighting a war to preserve or promote a religion.

But we like to blame our various religions for wars and conflicts and petty over-the-back-fence arguments. We draw real or imaginary lines to separate us from those with different religious beliefs, and even those who belong to the same religion but practice it differently. Is it the other person's spiritual life we seek to extinguish in these circumstances? Or is it the physical life? Do we seek to kill someone else because they wear, or do not wear, head coverings when they worship? Or maybe because they kneel a certain way, or not at all? Because they light candles, or shun them? Or because they believe their god lives in one place, and we believe ours lives in another?

No, we go to war for other reasons. The things we fight for, like the freedom to worship or go to school or work, may not be negative, but let's not fool ourselves by calling these wars "religious." We fight wars to satisfy our greed; we want what another group has, like territory or oil. We fight wars to seek revenge for some real or perceived injury or insult. We fight wars to defend ourselves from those who want what we have.

Sometimes the lines of conflict fall between differing religions; other times we may identify our enemies by politics, language, skin colour, or geography. But if those differences were reasons for war great nations could never exist, because they are made up of people with huge differences among them. And no one anywhere, at any time, would ever get along, become friends, love, or become part of a community or a nation, because we are all so different. If we are meant to self-destruct, so be it, we can continue our warring ways. Just don't blame God.

CRITICAL ONLOOKERS

When Mellisa Hollingsworth came within fractions of a second of winning a medal in the 2010 Olympic skeleton race, she cried. On camera. She didn't cry because she'd lost. She didn't cry because her feelings were hurt. She cried because she felt like she'd let down her country. If there was ever a time I wanted to reach into the TV screen to give someone a hug, it was right then. How could she imagine she'd let us down? She was already a medal winner, taking bronze four years earlier in Torino. She's a hero for sacrificing what most of us would call a normal life in order to represent a nation of couch potatoes for a few brief, head-first descents down a curled icicle. And she sets an example of good citizenship, because when she's not riding horses or training or hurtling downhill at illegal highway speeds on a skinny little sled, she's helping underprivileged youngsters.

No, Mellisa, you didn't let us down. It's the other way around, because your fellow Canadians have not made it plain that we're proud of you and other Olympians whether or not you win a medal. We armchair athletes have no basis to complain about your achievements. If we could do what you do, we would—and we don't. Let's face it: if we all played hockey like Sidney Crosby or snowboarded like Sarah Conrad, we'd not be sitting and watching. We'd be doing.

As in sports, so it is in life. It's easy to criticize someone else's lifestyle choices, work or relationships, decision-making or skills. It's much more difficult to actually do what that other person is doing. How many of us would want to make a life-and-death decision about removing even a tiny part of an organ from a sick person's body? Or study for the length of time it takes to learn how to perform surgery? Who wants to decide if it's better to lock someone up or give them one more try at rehabilitation? Who wants to choose between spending public money on a program for emerging artists or planting a tree downtown? Who among us wants to represent their peers in thankless political or volunteer positions? Or go out in a raging snowstorm to work on high-tension electrical wires? Or walk into the middle of violence to try to stop the fighting? Which one of us would like to live so close to the edge of survival that stealing food seems like a reasonable option? Who wants to be the person who feeds, clothes, shelters, educates, and counsels the people who need that kind of help? Who wants to be always ready to do any of these things at a moment's notice?

If we can do something and want to do it, we should. We all have a niche to fill, a purpose for being, and it's not to moan about someone else's performance while ignoring our own.

Most of us don't want to imagine what it's like to be someone else. It's much easier to criticize someone else's footwear than to walk in their shoes. Jesus Christ said it well: Take the big two-by-six timber out of your own eye before you start digging at your buddy's to get out the speck of sawdust. We are responsible for what we do, and for what we don't. As for the next fellow's burdens, why not help with the load instead of magnifying it? If we had a fraction of the sense of responsibility possessed by those Olympic athletes who keenly feel the weight of representing 30 million Canadians, the world would be a better place.

FICKLE IMPERFECTION

We humans have short attention spans. We enjoy our current circumstances, whatever they are, for only so long before we look for something new. That's why fashions change; newspapers, magazines, and websites constantly re-design themselves; television shows last only so many seasons; and radio stations change schedules. Culture industries cash in on our inclination to move on to the next big thing, whether it's because of changing demographics, times, morals, or needs. Change can be necessary and even good, but sometimes there is nothing wrong with the same old thing. Humans, like crows, are attracted by flash that has no substance.

People are tired of the same old religion. Check attendance at the so-called mainline churches. Think the stock market dipped? Take a look at the dive in traditional religious obser-vances. But humans aren't tired of the concepts of a supreme, living, and infinite creator, the existence of our own souls, the conflict between good and evil, or the presence of holiness. We just don't want to call it religion. The word raises images of institutions and organizations that have committed atroci-ties ranging from physical, emotional, economic, and political abuse and violence, to the use of absurd and tedious worship practice in order to suppress joy and curiosity. Religion, as we think of it today, has a lot to answer for.

It's interesting that "pious" was once the preferred word to describe anyone deeply involved in sacred life. That word now brings to mind a person who acts holy in public, and does God knows what in private. It's likely only a matter of time before the word spiritual also goes out of favour because the actions of a few taint the whole barrel.

Words are powerful, but they are just words (as comedian George Carlin pointed out in his monologue The Seven Dirty Words You Can't Say on Television). Words represent ideas, things, people, and actions that continue no matter what we call them.

No religion started out to be bad, but as a way to collect, preserve, and share wonderful and inspiring events and concepts. Unfortunately, humans are imperfect in our abilities to communicate and to understand, so we have not found the perfect description of the entity we often call God, or the sense of wholeness that comes from a truly spiritual experience that we may call grace, blessing, rapture, or transcendence. Over time, in a poor human effort to ensure the continuation of something that cannot be killed, we've made up silly rules and taken counterproductive measures to hang on to those wonderful and inspiring events and concepts. How else could the most excellent teachings of someone like Jesus or Mohammed, or any of the sages and prophets down through the ages, be used as an excuse for sexual abuse, war, treachery, racism, or other demonstrations of hatred? We do it when we try to box what has no bounds, and control what we cannot understand.

We can change the words, we can start anew every hour, but we can't change the essence of Creation: the living, moving breath of Life and Love that is greater than all of us put together but remains a personal Example and Goal for those who seek.

I capitalized those words on purpose. Substitute what you will.

SIN

As the Israelites were about to enter the Promised Land after wandering the desert for forty years, God told Joshua, "Today I have rolled away from you the disgrace of Egypt." The disgrace, or shame, was that the Israelites enabled the pharaohs to enslave them because they'd lost touch with God while living in Egypt. By the time Moses came along to lead the Israelites from slavery to the Promised Land, society treated them like dirt, and they felt like dirt.

Freedom from Egyptian persecution did not suddenly make the Israelites happy about wandering in the desert. No, they wanted to go back to Egypt where at least there was food. More than the whippings, the rapes, and the back-breaking work they had endured in captivity, they were frightened of the future. After generations of being told what to do, they didn't really know how to behave.

The Ten Commandments were meant to address that problem, but Moses was on the mountain for so long fetching them that his people thought he wasn't coming back. Out of ignorance and fear, they began to consult their old idols and good luck charms. Moses came down the mountain carrying the stone tablets that God had etched with the commandments, but he smashed them to pieces in rage when he saw what the Israelites were doing. Thankfully, God allowed Moses to make a new set.

The third commandment was broken, however, as soon as it was announced: "You shall not make for yourself a carved image, or any likeness of anything that is in heaven above, or that is in the earth beneath, or that is in the water under the earth. You shall not bow down to them or serve them, for I the LORD your God am a jealous God, visiting the sins of the fathers on the children to the third and the fourth generation of those who hate me."

Three or four generations will suffer for the sins of their ancestors. We know this is true. When someone commits murder, adultery, or theft, the children pay, as do their children and their children. When a person walks away from righteous teachings, their family suffers until the grandchildren or great-grandchildren come around on their own. It takes a long time for a family or a community to get over trauma, to get back on the right track, and start over.

God forgave the Israelites' sins as they entered the Promised Land, where they would start over. In our own lives, we do this over and over again. We admit we're wrong, we seek forgiveness, and we start over. But no matter how good we try to be, we all make mistakes. We need to recognize and acknowledge our wrongs, and we need to say, sorry, let's try that again.

Each of us is also sinned against, and put in the position of forgiving another person so he or she can start over and the world will be a better place for everyone. As in the Bible story of the runaway son (Luke 15), we all screw up. (It's a great story about a spendthrift son who wastes his inheritance living recklessly, until he hits rock bottom and decides to go home to Dad empty-handed. His ecstatic father welcomes him and provides for him—but there is a "good" brother who is not so happy. It's worth the read.) We fall for what makes us comfortable in the strange wilderness that the world often seems to be. We forget the habit of conversing with God. We do the easy, popular thing instead of the right, scary thing. Then, when we've worn out our last welcome, we want the chance to start over. Luke 15 tells us that yes, we can start over, but it's not easy.

We've all experienced insults and injury at the hands of others. Often, family and community close out the wrongdoer until someone breaks ranks and forgives the sinner. Some celebrate, and some, like the brother in the story, feel betrayed, because allies have seemingly switched sides. There is a man in the story who continues to resent the way his brother hurt him, and he can't bring himself to forgive him. The brother might feel better if the wrongdoer apologized out loud directly to him, instead of only to their father.

Christians traditionally apologize to the Father—to God—during formal confession. God hears the apology and forgives the sinner. But the person in the next pew may not hear the apology, and therefore may not have any reason to forgive. Similarly, I may hold a grudge for years, because I have no idea that the object of my grudge apologized to God a long time ago. He or she is moving on while I'm stuck in the past, all bent out of shape over a long-ago hurt.

The world would be better if we could accept that God knows what's in a person's heart even if we don't, that God will forgive. If we hold a grudge forever, are we not implying we know more than God? If God loved only people whom we judge to deserve it, we'd all go loveless. But God loves us freely, when we've gone missing, when we resent the happiness of others, when others think we're unlovable, when we're so ashamed of ourselves we squirm in the mirror, when we're just sin waiting to happen.

Trust is essential for getting on with life. Today it may be your brother who seeks forgiveness. Tomorrow it could be me or you. How do we want to be treated when it's our turn?

IT'S ALL ABOUT US

The beavers that adorn Canadian nickels, flood roads, and chew down ornamental trees have an unpleasant smell—and their ponds stink too. They have a slick, greased-down appearance and long, gross yellow teeth. They're an unlikely national symbol. But anyone who has ever watched a beaver build a dam, or who has tried to take one apart, can only stand in awe of what this little rodent can do. With nothing but sticks, rocks, mud, teeth, paws, and plenty of energy, a beaver can build a dam that holds backs tonnes of water. It can fell several cords of wood with its jaws and teeth and create ponds that rival water features coveted by subdivision designers. And if the beavers are still in residence, any breach in the dam is repaired overnight. They will even rebuild a dam after it's been cleared by a backhoe.

Compare that effort and ability to similar human endeavours. On one hand we have an animal that's related to the much-maligned rat, which can build a complicated structure as an innate response to the sound of running water. On the other, we have a brainy animal at the top of the food chain that requires heavy machinery and a lot of planning by engineers and architects to build a complicated structure.

The beaver probably cares as little about us as we do about it—unless we are suddenly thrust into each other's company. In such cases, the beaver would likely see humans as a threat, and we would view a beaver as a nuisance, a creature of little worth, something to capture and cart away to a place where it wouldn't interfere with our endeavours. That's the view we humans have with any part of Creation we don't like, whether it's animal, plant, human, or dirt. We seem to have an ingrained disability to marvel at anything that is not just like us, for which we can't immediately find a use, or that we can't claim as our own.

Whatever we have the power to do, we do it. We gobble up resources before someone else gets them. We get rid of anything and anybody that we don't like before they hurt us first. We scrape the earth bare and justify it by citing economic demands, so our forests disappear. When we eliminate dandelions from our lawns, we justify it by saying they threaten our property values—and then we replace them with exotic greenery shipped from afar aboard fuel-guzzling machinery. When we shun situations involving the unusual, the unsightly, or the unhealthy, we justify it by saying we're too busy and emotionally sensitive to handle it. Then we complain about being lonely and bored. We justify value by monetary worth, but some things that appear useless or even a nuisance will surprise us upon closer examination.

Instead of extorting every last nickel from Creation, we need to marvel at it, the big, the small, the weird, and even the seemingly ordinary, like the amazing rodent on our five-cent piece.

We think we're so smart, but we have an awful lot to learn.

PART IV

The Big Picture

LITTLE THINGS MATTER

Pick up one piece of a jigsaw and it doesn't make much sense. A swirl of green and a slash of black could be a piece of tree or a leprechaun, but you can't tell for sure until it gets fitted to another piece, and then another. If the completed puzzle is shown on the box, the picture helps us determine that the miniscule touch of red on the tab of a puzzle piece can only be the thumb of the little boy's mitten. Soon, its shape emerges.

Life is a puzzle, too. There are bits and pieces here and there that seem to have no connection or relationship to each other, and we have to figure out how to fit circumstances into our lives, and our lives into circumstances. Nothing seems straightforward. In school, learning to colour within the lines seemed like a tedious and silly thing to practice, but later we realized we were being trained in hand–eye coordination (and maybe some self-discipline). Generations of high school students have questioned the practical use of algebra or geography, only to discover a decade later that they should have paid more attention in class. Ultimately, it only makes sense when the pieces finally fit together.

Religious traditions, ethics, morals, and even good manners are among the lessons impressed on us as children that make no sense at the time. Being admonished for biting a sibling or showing off may enrage a toddler, but it serves as a useful lesson for getting along with other people. We learn the rules.

As we assemble our puzzle, we take all the straight edges and lay them out as a framework for the big picture. We say to ourselves, "This is the rule. This is the line over which we cannot and will not go." Unlike puzzle boxes, life doesn't come with a picture of the finished product; it emerges as we go along. The straightforward parts are the easiest and most logical place to start. Next, we work on a bunch of similarly coloured jigsaw pieces that fit together to form a house or a tree. In life, we focus on assembling an education or a family, or handling the details of a particular challenge. Satisfied that we've finished one part, we move to other pieces that seem to belong together.

But the puzzle is still a collection of highlights. Incomplete. To get the big picture, the monotonous little in-between bits have to be connected. They may be bland and uninteresting and hard to fit together, but they are significant because they anchor the rest of the pieces, give them place and meaning. These pieces are the small everyday acts of love, kindness, and caring responsibility that glue life together. They are the time, talents, or treasures that we share: the friendly word or smile, the offer of help, the shoulder to cry on, even our daily chores. They happen every day, so we sometimes think they don't count, but, if left out, our lives would have huge empty spaces.

RELIGION

Once upon a time, organized religion was responsible for the welfare of humanity. In primitive cultures—that is, cultures viewed as primitive from a twenty-first century perspective—there were religious or mystical figures whose duty it was to heal the sick. Whether these figures used herbal concoctions, chants, rudimentary surgery, fasting, or other processes, to the ordinary citizens of that time and place their work was a spiritual event. Medicine is still spiritual in many parts of the world, and to my mind these practices should not be automatically pooh-poohed as mere superstition. After all, many of our ancestors survived plagues and whatnot because of them. Fast-forward a bit, and we find religious orders operating hospitals, first-aid posts, and nursing homes.

In the good—or bad, depending on your perspective— old days, monks, nuns, clergy, or their equivalents taught children to grow up. Doses of religious belief were administered along with education in literacy, science, and math. Learning to read and write meant studying the wisdom of the ancestors, including various faith systems. Picture orange-robed, bald-shaven men bent over their studies; or a woman in head-to-toe black-and-white garb standing before a class of neatly combed and clad youngsters, their hands folded on their severe wooden desks; or well-wrapped figures seated on the ground. These pupils are all learning how to operate day-to-day in a secular world, but any observer with a grain of sense knows that they are likely absorbing the religious culture of their instructors as well.

Over the centuries, religious leaders of every stripe have urged followers to help the poor, feed the hungry, walk lightly on the earth, and be aware and in awe of the Creator. Religious groups organized to provide clothing and shelter to the homeless, open soup kitchens, make rules about when and how to plant and hunt, and provide places to worship. Body, mind, and soul: religion used to take care of all of it. But you can't run schools and hospitals and churches and shelters without staying on top of the paperwork. As the number of useful activities grew and more and more people became involved in religion, its leaders had to create guidelines or rules to help people live and work together in harmony. Then someone had to be designated to keep track of the rules and explain why they were introduced in the first place. Eventually, sanctions were established for disobeying the rules. In other words, to be able to handle it all, religion—or religions—had to get organized.

The term "organized religion" has since become dirty; it symbolizes to us all that goes wrong when we focus on maintaining the institution of religion rather than its purpose. As a result, there is a sense that the purpose of religion has been lost, leaving us with nothing more than an institution that bends itself double trying to maintain itself. Religions seem to have turned their backs on the world's needs, and denied their own teachings in the effort to sustain appearances. There is also a strong worldwide tradition of religions and government being one and the same: religious doctrine forms and influences government legislation, and vice versa. The tradition means that both state and religion have a vested interest in each other's survival, to the detriment of the religion's original, spiritual purpose.

Back in the day people would give their money and/or harvest to, say, a Christian church, in order to support its good works—operating orphanages, hospitals, schools, missions to the poor, and so on—as well as spread the message of Jesus Christ. While official state religions still exist in many nations, religion and state have parted ways in most of what we call the western world. Along with that division, and in order to make it fair for everyone in the country, religion gave up tasks like education, health care, shelter, and public welfare, and today we pay taxes instead of giving alms.

After handing over responsibility for mind and body to government, religion was left with matters of the soul. But in our daily lives, it's hard to separate soul from mind and body. It's not a bad thing that government cares for minds and bodies. It's not a bad thing for religions to care for souls. But we've got to get it together, if for no other reason than our survival. Humans come with mind, body, and soul in the same package, and we work better when we keep it that way. Nations might work better, too, with a cohesive approach. If any government could officially recognize that spirituality or religion is as important to people as health and education, without favouring one particular brand over another, the nation's citizens would have less to fear from their differences. Any battle over religious supremacy would cease to have a purpose in that country. And other nations will follow suit.

If we focus on how we are alike instead of how we are different, maybe we can come up with a way for religion to wrap its arms around government, and for government to make room for religions. Maybe it will be something God will like.

THE AIR WE BREATHE

So we're jogging along in life as usual, taking for granted such niceties as heat or light or water, when up swoops this weather system thousands of kilometres south of us, over warm water. It wreaks havoc long before it gets to us, where it inconveniently knocks down trees and power lines, causes floods, and strips off roofs and siding. So much for advanced civilization. Just like ancient times, it's dark after sunset and cold when the fire goes out. But however bad it gets, here in Canada we can usually compare our property loss and power outages to the destruction in other places and feel quite safe.

To listen to the roaring wind and feel its power, and then escape safely, makes a person a bit more sympathetic to those who endured the worst of the storm as it peaked in the tropics. For a few days, these are not just people in a far-off place enduring the hardships that we see on television. They are neighbours, making their way through the same storm as we are.

Aren't we all in the same tempest? Don't we all breathe the same air?

The atmosphere surrounding the planet just goes in circles, with bubbles of air and dust and water vapour arriving in Nova Scotia from Ontario or New England today, before heading towards Newfoundland tomorrow and then on towards Ireland the next. By this time next week or next month we might be inhaling some of the stuff we exhaled last Sunday—who knows?

I've heard it said that DNA from the Egyptian pharaohs could be found in the dust of the air we breathe today—if one was inclined to look for it. If this is true, then presumably we can also find genetic material from Moses or Sir John A. Macdonald or Shakespeare or Hitler, as well as billions of Earth's more obscure citizens. That makes each of us a conglomeration of everything that has gone before us. It means that the bits that make us are shared among other members of Creation existing with us here on earth today. It means that we, and other living things, are contributing to the future, even if it is eons away.

That's a bit scary, to think that something we do here today can affect someone else, somewhere else, next month or next millennium. It's a vast responsibility, too huge to contemplate most of the time. So we don't think about it, until something happens that makes us feel connected to a part of the human family that's otherwise distant in time or place. Normally, we care only superficially if there's a flood here, an earthquake there, a famine somewhere, or war anywhere. But if the flood happens in the village where our grandparents were born we pay more attention, and we may try to help those affected. If the earthquake occurs where we vacationed last year, we notice, and we may feel some responsibility to the community. A famine may mean nothing to us until we see an image of a starving infant and realize he or she could be one of our own children. There is always war somewhere, so we grow indifferent—until our sons and daughters and brothers and sisters go off to fight in it.

While it's unnerving to realize that, for instance, the well-intentioned chemical we use today could injure future generations, or that our eating habits at home could hurt someone on the other side of the Earth, there is also a comfort in being part and parcel of everything that exists.

It shows we are not alone.

Every single one of us is part of the global community, and each of us has a function in the world. Whatever we do, no matter how small or seemingly unimportant at the time, has an effect on someone or somewhere else. And what other people do affects each of us. So it's a good thing to be good to each other, because it's a small world—and it's getting smaller.

LISTEN

A friend of mine recently served as a delegate to a large gathering of her church whose attendees included people from other communities in the region and from farther afield. Prior to the meeting, she and other delegates held "boring" (her word!) meetings about what they would do and say at the larger conference. They studied and discussed the issues so they could be prepared. It was all very *we must do this because somebody has to* ho-hum.

She assumed the large gathering would be the same: staid and dutiful, with a lot of talk. She was totally unprepared to be interested in or excited about the proceedings. Imagine her surprise when she discovered that the energy of hundreds of other delegates galvanized her, piquing her interest in issues that had hitherto seemed distant and unconnected. The wide array of topics, the reams of information, and the involvement of people of all ages and walks of life served as "a real eye-opener," she said. She had prepared to vote a certain way on the issues presented at the meeting, but found that her point of view changed as the gathering progressed. "You think you have your mind made up," she said, "and then you hear what other people have to say, and it makes you look at things differently."

Few wiser things have ever been said. Listening to the voices of others, really hearing their concerns, and working on understanding them, challenges our ideas, and, very often, changes us. It's so easy to get caught up in our own small corner of the world and lose sight of the larger picture.

Our own small corner is just as important as any other. But we may never find that out unless we reach out to the folks in those other small corners.

It's easy to dismiss or discount someone if you have never met them. We dismiss whole groups of people because of the place where they live, their skin colour, their accents, their jobs, their lifestyles, or their income. We rarely think of them, but if we do we lump them together. We are all guilty. We may pride ourselves on being non-racist, but dislike hearing a strange accent from a telemarketer. We may boast an attitude of equality, and never notice the garbage collectors until they go on strike. We may say we accept homosexuality, as long as our minister is not gay. We may sympathize with the sick, and dismiss drug addicts as deserving of their pain.

But our attitudes change if someone with an unfamiliar accent or skin colour marries into our family, or if a relative declares his or her homosexuality, or a son or daughter struggles with addiction. Then we sit up and take notice, and we find ourselves seeing the world through the other person's eyes. We stop measuring others by who *we* are, and learn to accept them as *they* are. The process requires an open mind and a loving heart, as well as the imagination to picture oneself in someone else's shoes, and the courage to reach out to the unknown.

We think we have our minds made up. But things are not always what they seem.

WE'RE ALL HERE TOGETHER

"It's the Birth of a New Tradition" headlines a new-millennial lobby to buy Canadian at Christmas. "Let's give the gift of genuine concern for other Canadians this Christmas," says the writer of an unsigned email that begins making the rounds in early November. Such a policy would provide local employment and improve the economy, they argue.

It's hard to know who "they" are, but it appears that this message began in the United States and was adapted for Canadian readers. According to my (limited) research, it's possible that the email began with the American Tea Party. Whoever wrote it managed to strum chords across the political spectrum. A message about shopping local and toning down the glitter appeals to the newly cash-strapped, those jaded by Christmas commercialism.

"Let's give gifts made by Canadian hands…. This is a revolution of caring about each other, and isn't that what Christmas is about?" However, the revolution doesn't apply if you are Chinese. The same email suggests a boycott of goods manufactured elsewhere, especially in China. If it weren't racist, xenophobic, and hypocritical, the message would be worth a snicker or two.

It is not "the birth of a new tradition." From its beginnings, Christmas was about love, or, to borrow the phraseology of this email, "a revolution of caring about each other." Christians know that the Christmas season celebrates the arrival of God in human form, an unprecedented gift that promotes the revolutionary notion of love in the face of hate and forgiveness in the face of hurt. Even people with no experience of its religious background have enjoyed the feel-good aspect of Christmas for as many years as they have denounced the long-established greed that threatens it. It's encouraging that successive waves of humanity yearn for a simpler Christmas, but there is more to it than buying local. Part of the larger picture—Christ's tall order—is that we care for everyone. That includes Chinese people.

Capitalist democracies complained for years about global communist threats, but when a country embraces capitalism well, the West cringes in fear. Using Christmas as an excuse to promote that fear for economic reasons is just wrong. Chinese factories churn out Christmas junk for us because, A: we like it and want to have it cheaply; and B: Western companies send manufacturing jobs to places with lower wages and fewer employee benefits to satisfy their shareholders (just check your pension plan's mutual funds). Meanwhile, in response to the message to tone down Christmas and boycott imported strings of lights and flat-screen TVs, some how-to gurus have offered directions for making gifts at home. Ironically, they suggest using materials imported from China.

Few Canadians would turn down a job with the potential to improve their personal and national economic situation, so why should we expect the Chinese to do so? True gifts should be presented cheerfully and lovingly from the heart, whether that involves shopping locally or ordering something from the other side of the world. A gift is about love for the recipient, not bragging rights for the giver. A gift involves thought, an examination of the heart that's doing the giving, and care for the person receiving it.

RESPONSIBILITY

The 2012 shooting deaths at Sandy Hook Elementary school in Newtown, Connecticut, were, and remain, a tragedy, a disaster, and a horror. There are not enough words to name the terror among those children and teachers as the shooting began. Nor is there enough room in our imaginations, stretched wide as they can be, to accommodate their experiences. Whatever we believe happened to the souls of these children—or their spirits, or the energy that was uniquely them—after they died does not change anything for them; they are beyond our reach. We, on the other hand, are still here. We react, grieve, and seek answers. And we say, Where was God when all this happened?

The slick answer to that is another question: Where were *we* when all this happened? And "all this" means every tiny or big event, every nuance of love or hate. Everything that happens has an effect. In the same way that shifting tectonic plates cause buildings to fall down along fault lines, and the sun's rays on Earth can result in either drought or harvest, the universe is designed to work, and we are part of it. We have control over our own choices, and that's about it.

After the Newtown shooting, the international media tracked down experts on mental illness, gun control, school security, and post-traumatic stress disorder. Instead of watching like noddy-dogs in the back of a Buick, we should examine our own roles when things go wrong for other people. Our actions and statements influence others, for better or for worse. How do we treat people behaving strangely, or those who are different? Can our actions today add to someone's growing disillusionment or anger, which may one day burst violently? Can our action or inaction prevent someone from getting the help that he or she needs? Can our sheep-like willingness to bow to the economic or political status quo prevent necessary change for the better?

The school shooting took place in December, so as well as pondering God's whereabouts, we grieved for Christmas. But tragedies occur every December. The 2012 Bangladesh factory fire, the wreck of an Australian fishing boat filled with refugees in 2010, the 2004 Boxing Day tsunami, the 1989 murders at l'École Polytechnique in Montreal, the 1917 Halifax Explosion, and a 1907 methane explosion in a West Virginia coal mine: altogether these tragedies killed more than 232,000 people, all in the weeks around Christmas. And each victim's death was significant to the people who loved them.

No one expected the shootings in Newtown, a picture-perfect place. But things were not perfect for one young man, and because of that, life is even less perfect for at least thirty more families. As time goes by other tragedies clutch our attention, and we forget to worry about what will happen to the mothers, fathers, brothers, and sisters of those children and adults who died. The question for each of us remains: where are *we* in all this? What is our role? It is a God-given choice, not one forced upon us: we can focus on loving each other, an activity that we can practice and an attitude we can nurture with hope and faith. We can start there any time.

THE VILLAGE STANDARD

We are not alone. For the purposes of this book, that's not a statement of belief in the existence, or lack thereof, of extraterrestrial life or a supreme being. It's just the bald fact that we share this planet with billions of other people, not to mention animals and plants. We haven't yet achieved the technology to load two of everything into a space-ark for an intergalactic tour while we wait for the Earth's wounds to heal, so we're stuck with each other. As the world's population grows, the space between us gets smaller and smaller.

Once upon a time here in Canada, one could travel a long way out of town before coming to the next place. Now, we hardly ever get out of sight of human occupation—and just try to find a patch of virgin forest or untouched shoreline. Even in the midst of areas apparently void of humans, we come across a pop can or a fence post—and this is Canada, a country with vast areas of wilderness. Imagine what it's like in more densely populated nations.

The relatives of US President Barack Obama live in a once-remote African village, a place we might never have seen except that its images were flashed around the world on the day Obama was elected. The food in our cupboard no longer comes from the patch behind the house or the farm down the road. It comes from across the world, produced by people we'll never meet. (On the other hand, maybe we will meet them. It's no surprise any more to discover in casual conversation with a stranger that he or she is a distant relative, or that we share a handful of mutual friends or a favourite coffee shop.)

Anyone who lives in a small community knows that you can't say anything about anybody, because everyone will know. So you keep your mouth shut and mind your manners, unless you want to flee to another community. Trouble is, even the farthest ends of the earth are almost next door. So as the global village shrinks, maybe it's time to adopt the village standard of putting up with each other's idiosyncrasies. And that includes our religious differences.

In a really big world, we could each have a special corner to live out our faith however we want, with no fear of interfering or being interfered with. But as we get pressed into smaller spaces, we struggle to maintain our distances psychologically and emotionally rather than physically. We avoid contact to pretend we still have space, and we make up new rules of engagement to protect ourselves from the threats of open and honest dialogue.

New ideas challenge the notion that ours is the only way, until even those faith systems that assume exclusive rights to specific states and nations have to sink or swim in the widening pool of religious possibilities. We tend to cling to our traditions, but they often have little to do with the core of our professed faith. For example, if we believe that God created the earth and everything in it, does that change if we celebrate it a different way? If we believe in loving others as we want to be loved, as most religions teach, we have to make room. Because we're not alone.

SIGNS AND SYMBOLS

The date February 15, 1965, sticks in my head. It was the day that everyone in my school got a white pencil with a tiny maple leaf flag painted on it near the eraser end. Because of that pencil, I remember the day Canada got its own flag.

I kept the pencil for a long time, and wouldn't even use it because I was so proud of the flag. It was the first flag that was really mine, as a Canadian. Before that we had the red ensign, to me a sort of hand-me-down British flag, that they didn't use much. I knew I was Canadian, not British or American or anything else, even though my family background was a mishmash of various cultures. I believed that Canada was the best place in the world but, to tell the truth, I'd never been anywhere else. I've travelled a bit since then and I'm still proud of my country.

My family moved three times after 1965, but I held on to my flag pencil. Then in the 2000s, someone in the house needed a pencil—and that was the end of it. I don't even have a stub of that pencil any more.

I've since figured out that I don't need that particular pencil, because there are plenty of them in the world (although apparently not in my house on that particular day). I also figured out that I don't need that particular flag on that particular pencil. We fly our Maple Leaf wherever and whenever we can. I looked out a hotel window in Halifax one time to see six Canadian flags flying on six separate buildings in one short block. I see it on lapel pins, on books and documents and backpacks, and I've even seen it on bottles of laundry detergent.

My flag pencil served its purpose, by reminding me for most of my life that Canada is an independent country, with a unique culture and a magnificent land. It reminded me that Canadians are basically good and fair and, if there is something I don't like, I have the freedom to say so and to work to rectify the situation.

I'm not going to forget all that, pencil or no pencil. Flag or no flag.

I can draw a picture of the Canadian flag with my eyes closed, but sometimes it's a little harder to think about what the flag represents. While I understand and support an attitude of respect for our flag, it's not the Maple Leaf that is the most important. It's not the fabric or paper and paint or dye of which the flag is made, it's what our flag stands for. It reminds us of the best and most desirable aspects of Canada, and also of issues in our country that need to be improved upon, and that we, as Canadians, are responsible for that.

But that's the purpose of a flag—to be a symbol. The Maple Leaf joins other flags from other countries as symbols of people and nations around the world. And flags are just one kind of symbol. Religion is rife with symbols, often because of persecution that forces people to worship in secret for fear of discrimination, torture, or even death. A simple fish drawing is now a well-known Christian symbol, but it was once a secret sign among persecuted believers.

The Star of David was used in the 1930s and 1940s by the Nazis to identify Jewish citizens so they could be robbed, displaced, and eventually tortured and killed in death camps, during what we now call the Holocaust. The blue-and-white symbol later became the flag of the Jewish state of Israel, but the six-pointed star and hexagram from which it is derived are also shared by Hinduism and Wicca (and maybe more). Islam's flowing calligraphic rendition of "Allah" is just one example of a religion using words or letters to share the faith.

Primitive religions chose symbols from nature, like plants or celestial images. Various forms of crosses date back to earliest pagan rituals, long before Jesus was crucified on one. Circular shapes, found in ancient gravesites and believed to represent the cycle of life and the seasons, turn up today as wreaths or other emblems. Images of holy people, triangles, lambs, eagles, hearts, anchors, roses, grapes, bread, doves, mazes, lilies, swords, knots, wreaths, rainbows, flames, kites, salt, tree roots, candles, holly, cups, coloured powder—these are all symbols for one kind of religion or another. Special haircuts, clothing and jewelry, places, hand gestures, and body postures also serve as symbols and aids for worship. These things generally represent how our spiritual lives and the divine are intertwined with our everyday physical existence, but what is spiritually significant for some can be an object of curiosity or even scorn for others.

Some of us venerate objects as representations of God and believe they have powerful Godly characteristics; some use them as reminders of God; some get to God without symbols; some don't get to God at all. We carry four-leaf clovers, check our horoscopes, examine runes, genuflect according to our various religious upbringings, and seek spiritual meaning in trivial everyday events or objects. Like a flag, they remind us of something greater than ourselves. We rely on our symbols to prod our feelings, our spirits, and our approach to the divine.

But still, we wonder, can an important Christian symbol like the cross have any real power for a non-Christian? Does

Jerusalem have as much importance to a Druid as to a Jew? Can the written invocation of the name of Allah mean anything to a non-Muslim? Does a pyramid or a crystal or a lucky number have any effect on someone who doesn't believe in their benefits?

Do religious signs and symbols have any power in and of themselves, or are they important because they remind us what truly is?

GOD IN A BOX

A recent television program showed salvage hunters scouring an abandoned church building to collect items of value before a wrecking ball reduced the place to rubble. Formerly the centre of a thriving neighbourhood, the church and its membership dwindled as people migrated to the suburbs. Finally, when its large worship space, auditorium, offices, gymnasium, and living accommodations fell empty, the few remaining congregants had the task of deciding what to do with the leftovers of a once-vibrant community. Everything was up for grabs, from ornately carved pews and immense stained-glass windows to old-fashioned exercise equipment and the tinwork on the ceilings. The physical remnants of generations who had given their time, talent, and treasure to create something beautiful for God, were soon to be nothing but dust.

It's happening everywhere.

Look around to see unused church buildings turned into homes, cottages, art galleries, libraries, studios, garages, daycare centres, stores and, occasionally, worship spaces for different faith traditions. Young people raised in local churches move away and don't come back, while their aging parents and grandparents struggle to keep these barn-like structures warm, painted, and insured—and to pay a living wage to clergy—all so that the building can be occupied for a couple of hours a week. People new to communities tend not to attach themselves to churches, especially if they think they will be expected to maintain buildings rather than feed their spirits.

Closing a church building means people learn to worship in an unaccustomed way in a different place—if they continue to worship at all. But the early church, back in the first and second century, worshipped in homes, ships, and restaurants. The first European settlers to Canada did the same. Many of us today have worshipped in gyms, kitchens, living rooms, fire halls, classrooms, libraries, and even outdoors. In my experience, it matters less where worship is, than that it takes place at all.

Churches thrive when they can focus on worship rather than on buildings—either because they have no financial worries or because they have no building. But most congregations have inherited from previous generations the pointy structures, special furniture, linens, candlesticks, and all the other accoutrements once deemed necessary for proper worship. Each succeeding generation does its best to be faithful to that trust, but there inevitably comes a point where stained glass and polished brass become burdens rather than cherished treasures. And then what happens?

As Jesus suggested to the rich man, the church could sell its wealth, give the money to the poor, and dance off in freedom to love and serve God. Or the church could hang on to its wealth in the hopes that taking care of oak and linen will get folks into heaven, a probability once famously compared to guiding a camel through the eye of a needle.

If the buildings are gone, where will people meet for worship? A passerby is not likely to drop into a stranger's house or a fire hall on the remote chance that someone might be worshipping within—even on a Sunday.

How will we know where to find God?

God is not hiding in a box or a particular building—although you might find God there or anywhere else, any time, even after all the buildings fall down and the art turns to dust.

UP CLOSE AND PERSONAL

My niece got married in an outdoor religious ceremony beside the sea. It rained a bit, just little spits that failed to smear the ink on the marriage documents. The bride was beautiful and the groom was handsome. The overcast sky was perfect for photography, and the dresses, the flowers, the decorations, and the food were all appropriately lovely. People shed tears, as is done at weddings, and they laughed and sang and danced and gabbed. As modern weddings go, it was simple as well as sincere, relaxed, and fun. But the best thing by far was the obvious acceptance by all concerned that the wedding wasn't about a ceremony and a reception. It was about a marriage: the days and years to come.

Marriage is a commitment to share the future, whatever it may bring. That's a bit scary, because none of us knows what the future holds. When we marry, we don't know our spouse well enough to predict whether he or she will be weak or strong in situations that we can't begin to imagine. How will he or she react to illness, job loss, infidelity, irritability, addiction, violence, poverty, sorrow, natural disasters, sexual dysfunction, property loss, the demands of extended family and the community, child-rearing issues, obsessions, physical separation, or any number of other distractions? The average two and a half years of courtship is not long enough to find out. And maybe that's a good thing.

On our wedding day, we cannot foresee the challenges that will try our patience, our pocketbooks, and our love for each other. At times the only thing holding two people together might be the promises made at their wedding: to stick together in the face of adversity because their love for each other will overcome whatever life may throw at them. When that love seems distant, remembering those vows can get a couple through a sticky few minutes, days, or even months.

Marriage is a joy and a blessing, but it's for grown-ups, not wimps. A wedding is not a frivolous undertaking carried out for the sake of the cake and costumes. If it were simply an excuse for a party, the union of two people's hearts and minds and bodies would matter no more to religious and secular governments than if the same couple passed each other on the sidewalk. Marriage is not important because religious tradition, tax law, financial transactions, and medical records all pay attention to one's marital status. It is the other way around: society pays attention because marriage is important. It's the basic unit of the family, and the concept of family is the building block of nations.

Whether a couple is married by a religious service, joined in a civil ceremony, or privately committed to each other through common law, the union is a holy one that deserves and needs the support of family and community. If the Creator has joined two people, it cannot be our puny human duty to oppose the union. A marriage may be a mistake from the get-go and doomed to divorce; or, more happily, couples may have the love, courage, and honesty to share their imperfections as well as their attributes. Their relationship is their responsibility. That they may live in a culture of love and support is the responsibility of the rest of us.

POVERTY AND PLUTOCRACY

In 2010 McGill University Professor of Economics Thomas Velk spoke up against a governmental initiative to give tax breaks to low-income earners, a move suggested by Toronto-Dominion Bank Chief Executive Ed Clark as a way to stimulate the economy. Velk said that money should go instead to productive citizens: Canada doesn't "need to give money to beer drinkers," Velk said.

In trickle-down economics, the rich get richer and can therefore hire more poor people for menial labour. The model didn't work well for Louis XVI, who notoriously lost his head when his nation's beer-drinking equivalents held a much-celebrated revolution; it didn't work well in more recent years in Haiti or North Korea; and it isn't likely to work well in modern Canada. But that's just my mildly held opinion on supply-side economics. My outrage at bigotry is something else again.

Velk at least had the guts to say what many others were merely thinking. But his comment demonstrates an ever-increasing attitude among policy-makers, that low-income Canadians deserve their lot because of their lifestyle choices.

Clark and Velk were discussing tax breaks, indicating that the unproductive "beer-drinkers" in question earn enough to pay taxes, but not enough to enjoy, say, champagne or Scotch. That encompasses a lot of Canadians. If low-wage earners chose another drink over beer, would this school of thought offer them a tax break?

My guess is no. If the stereotype were of a milk-drinking lower class, Velk's crowd would argue against tax breaks for milk-drinkers. It's not about the beverage; it's about the power.

Lots of wealthy people drink beer or whatever they please, sometimes to excess. Just like their less-moneyed counterparts, they may do drugs and even sell them. They may gamble, likely for bigger stakes. They can have children out of wedlock and belong to dysfunctional families. They may drop out of school to work with Mom or Dad. They can be injured at war or at work, they can be mentally or physically ill, and they can be criminals. Rich people can make as many poor lifestyle choices as poor people—and more, given the options afforded by wealth. But none of it matters because they have money, and Velk and company wanted to give them more. The notion that low-income earners are less productive is a distraction. Countries and corporations cannot be run without labour. Whatever they drink, ordinary hardworking people don't deserve to be treated like a dreaded disease by their well-paid and well-pensioned government. The poor and the plutocrat stand equally before our Creator, naked of wealth, drink preferences, and political allegiances.

BLESSINGS

Outside my door there's a wheelbarrow heaped with muddy, wet carrots of every size and imaginable shape. It's a daunting prospect to clean, dry, and sort them: the small, twisted, and bug-attacked specimens into one bag to eat soon; the long straight carrots to be peeled, washed, sliced, blanched, rinsed, cooled, drained, and packed into bags for the freezer; and the rest into cold storage. It means hours and hours of tedious mind-numbing work, probably late into the night. It's the kind of job that makes a body tire to think about. On the other hand, there is a wheelbarrow full of fresh, organic carrots outside my door. They've been grown here to eat here and they'll likely last all winter. How many people are that lucky?

Nothing is free. Every good thing comes with a price, whether it's the sweat of our brows, or the money earned by hard work. We can complain about the price. On the other hand, we can do without and complain instead about that. Part of the trouble with planting, growing, digging, cleaning, processing, and storing carrots is that the work seems harder as I get older. It's easy to complain about the aching joints and sore feet and diminishing energy that come with age. But consider the alternative. Instead of growing old, I could be dying young. Looking at it this way makes me welcome every birthday.

Everything depends on viewpoint. We can complain about the car breaking down, but there are so many people in the world who don't have a car, and they get by. We complain about slow Internet connections, power outages, long waits at the hospital emergency department, the price of gasoline, the weather, slippery roads, the latest rounds of the flu, taxes, bills, homework, house-cleaning, nothing to watch on television, no money for vacation, post-Christmas doldrums—name it, and we can find something wrong with it. Aren't we just the picture of woe?

Except most of us have no experience with real woe.

So switch it around. Most people in the world don't have telephones, never mind computers or eight hundred channels on television, and they survive. Electricity and vacations are unheard-of luxuries in much of the world. Our health care is more advanced than it's ever been—and includes flu shots. Beer is expensive, too, but not many complain about that. Changing weather makes life interesting and gives us something to talk about when we meet new people.

Thank God for people who keep their illnesses to themselves, and for minds that brought us the telephone so we can talk to sick friends without exchanging germs.

Daring to complain about the bills we piled up ourselves ignores the free lesson for next year: don't do it. Some folks have to pay for courses in personal money management, but we've escaped tuition fees. If we earned or owned nothing, we could avoid taxes. So, aren't we lucky? And because we pay taxes, we have benefits like roads, health care, and education. They're not perfect (nothing is), but they exist, making us among the world's luckiest people.

There are folks who would enjoy having a house to clean, lessons to study, television, books, games, and something—anything—to do, and the wherewithal to do it. We don't really want to change places with them. We just like to complain.

If our wealth makes us unhappy, we can always give it away and concentrate on wonders like sunshine on snow or the roar of the wind through the sky—how can the invisible make so much noise? Inhale the aroma when someone comes in from outdoors: that smell doesn't come in a can! Feel the wonder and warmth of human contact, flesh on flesh, and pity the poor porcupine. Add up the good stuff.

Our satisfaction levels all depend on how we look at our lives—is the glass half full, or half empty? As the song says, "count your blessings, name them one by one, and it will surprise you what the Lord has done."

In my experience, it is an empowering exercise to tot up the good things in life. It would be interesting to scientifically examine the psychological and social benefits of counting blessings, to see if it helps heal bitterness, pervading sorrow, anger, jealousy, and a whole bunch of negative emotions.

Without that evidence, all one can say is that it's worth a shot to try thankfulness.

WHY (NOT) ME, LORD?

My knowledge of meteorology would fit in a thimble, but it seems that our weather on the Atlantic coast mostly comes from the west. Ottawa temperatures of two days ago will likely arrive on the east coast today, and if it's raining in Yarmouth in the morning, Antigonish folks will probably get wet before midnight. Weather systems also head up the American east coast, bringing hurricanes to Atlantic Canada in summer and sticky snowstorms in winter. And sometimes a mischievous system travels north of the Gulf of St. Lawrence and then swoops southward.

If all we can see is how the grass and trees bend, we might believe that the rain or snow or sunshine comes from the same direction as the wind. If all we know is that clouds are drifting northward across the sky, we might think we're about to breathe the air of our southern neighbours. But when we look at a satellite or radar image, we can see that the balmy south wind is part of a system that spun across the prairies last weekend, while a north wind chilled Chicago folks a few days ago. We can see how clear blue skies are pushed ahead of hurricanes, themselves born off the coast of Africa, to swirl across the south Atlantic to the Caribbean, and then northward towards Nova Scotia.

The big picture shows us where weather systems are formed, where they go, and where they might go next. The weather in our own little neighbourhood is affected by events far away, by the earth's rotation and its tour around the sun, and—I'm guessing here—by galactic events we've never even contemplated.

Just about everyone recognizes that, despite twenty-first-century technology, weather forecasting remains an inexact science. Rain falls on the just and the unjust and we only half-understand why. Yet we expect each of our personal lives to conform to our precious little understanding of how the universe works. When it doesn't, we cry that it's not fair, and we get angry with God. We ask, Why me? Why does God let people suffer? Why do bad things happen to good people? That cry is heard following every kind of upset, from lost car keys to multiple simultaneous fatalities. Thankfully my smart-mouth answer usually remains unvoiced. It goes like this: Why *not* me, or you? Why can't it happen to us? How can anyone be so special that nothing bad or upsetting or frustrating or sad ever, ever happens to them? People like that just don't exist. Into every life some rain must fall.

But I don't say all that, because when the sky is falling, no one, even me, wants to listen. And it's not really an answer to the eternal question, Why?

The answer is in the big picture, like a radar or satellite image of everything that was and is and will be. It's a big map of our actions and emotions, our physical and spiritual lives, our interactions with each other and the rest of Creation, and everything else that makes us, us. We're all born and we all die, some sooner and some later. In between, there are rose gardens and beds of nails. What comes before or after, we don't know. We have theories. We have beliefs. But as certain as they are, they are ours, not everyone's.

Bad things happen to good people and good things happen to bad people. But who decides who or what is good or bad? We can say a sudden death in the family is bad or tragic—and yes, it may be. But is it more tragic than a long, painful death? How do we know? What gives us the authority to decide?

We like to believe we have some control over our own futures—and in order to maintain some semblance of sanity, we live as if we really do. We take care of our health, look after our families, and squirrel away resources for the hard times. We can do everything correctly, and then wham! Disease, disaster, job loss, jail—something happens to upset our apple carts. Devastated, we holler, Why? Why me, Lord? Maybe someday we'll know why. Meanwhile, there will be tears in life, and there will be joy. So the answer becomes a matter of faith.

PART V
Our Gift to God

SACRIFICE

When I was a little kid, we had to march in pairs from our community school to the cenotaph every November 11, a distance of about three blocks. What I remember most is the weather. It almost always snowed big, soggy flurries that went right down our necks as we stood for two solemn minutes of silence. If we were caught twitching or sneezing or sniffing, we were in danger of detention or writing lines when we got back to school. My second most enduring memory is of hearing the "Last Post" and "Reveille" played scratchily over a car-mounted speaker, because no one in the community could play a real trumpet.

We didn't get a day off school (and children in that part of Canada still don't), but we didn't complain about our memorial duty. "The War" was all too recent in the memories of the most important people in our young lives: our parents. The veterans were our dads and, occasionally, our moms, and they were quite a bit younger than I am now.

During the ceremony, some of the veterans would blame the snow for the wetness on their cheeks; others would unashamedly pull out big white cotton hankies and blow their noses and wipe their eyes; still others stared sternly into space with their jaws bunched. They didn't have Critical Incident Stress Debriefing in those days. Some of the veterans talked about their experiences until their kids were sick of hearing, "When I was in the war…." Others never said a word, even when asked about their scars, or missing limbs, eyes, or fingers.

As much as the adventure aspect of war has been glorified on screen and in print, and as much as we envy and admire the camaraderie of those who served, it's hard to imagine that killing or waiting to be killed could be entertaining, or even noble. Instead, it always struck me that war must be a bit like those Remembrance Days of my youth: gray and miserable and tense and bitter, with fleeting patches of sunshine or blue sky enhancing the gleam of tears. To me, it was entirely appropriate that Remembrance Day came in November.

Once November 11 was over we got on with our lives, just like the war veterans had to when they came home from "over there." Unlike us, however, they had a store of memories that no amount of ceremony could entirely ease, or erase. But one thing those experiences must have taught them was that, although you can come awfully close, you can really die only once. And I'm told there's nothing like staring death in the face to sharpen your focus in life.

If you can escape someone's determined effort to kill you in an overseas war, what have you to fear when home among family and friends? Why not, then, speak out against injustice or injury? Why not take a leading role in community affairs? So, they did. First these men and women fought wars in faraway places so we could freely vote, work, travel, go to school and church, marry, run for political office, go on strike, and a whole bunch of other things we take for granted. Then they came home and worked hard to prosper their families, their communities, and their country.

Imagine. Our veterans paid an awful price for the society we are lucky to be part of, regardless of its faults. All their lives they cherished it, cared for it, improved it, and kept it in the best condition their resources allowed. Now it's up to their kids and grandkids to look after it. Please don't tell me we're too lazy and self-absorbed to handle this responsibility, or so stupid that we'd sell it to the highest bidder. It's guaranteed that someone, somewhere, would be ready to die for it.

LOVED AND LOVING

Maybe Judy could walk a long time ago, but I don't remember. I did see her dance a couple of times in the thirty years of our acquaintance. When she was younger, her dancing partner would bear her weight—about equal to dandelion fluff—and they'd sway to the music. Later, she'd rock her wheelchair to the beat and smile and smile. The medical community tried to help Judy walk, and the only time I saw her bitter about her lot in life was when a promising treatment actually worsened her situation. But limited physical mobility didn't prevent her from moving past that emotional challenge, to again become a delight to her family and friends. Once Judy, loving and loved, moved on for the last time, I pictured her kicking up her heels in the dance halls of heaven, no longer constrained by unresponsive nerves and muscles.

There are a lot of Judys in this world. The celebration of a child's birth is followed by dismay or alarm when her family realizes that things are not going as expected. They realize that a baby born with impaired mobility or mental capacity, or with other severe health issues, can mean a long, difficult road ahead. They see that raising this child will not offer the usual parental experience; they will be unable to watch her learn to crawl and walk and run and talk and grow up and leave home, and eventually bring back babies of her own.

There is sometimes a temptation to write off this new little person—lock her up, send her away, pretend she doesn't exist. Her intense and long-term care looms as an insurmountable obstacle that some families cannot face. It's a cold, hard fact that many people do not have the emotional, spiritual, or physical capability to handle another person's basic needs—any more than people in Judy's situation can care for themselves—and to try to do so could be harmful. For others, hands-on, at-home care is the only way.

There is no one-size-fits-all solution to long-term care for children with disabilities, or for aging and infirm parents, spouses, or siblings. So there can be no "they shoulda done this" or "They oughta do that" coming from onlookers: today it's them, but tomorrow it could be us. Someone—I think it was Winston Churchill—said that a society is measured by how it cares for its weakest members. That means none of us are off the hook. If a family or individual caregiver does not have the resources to care for a child who may never walk or talk, or a spouse lost in the mist of Alzheimer's, it is up to the rest of us to help. Whether we do so through our tax system or our own personal charity is a choice we are lucky to have.

We often question the value of a life that is maintained only by constant and close care and support. We ponder whether it's right or wrong to turn off machinery that keeps hearts and lungs working, to slip a fatal dosage to a terminally ill and pain-filled patient, or abort a potentially defective fetus. As in most situations, where people stand on the issue depends on what they see from where they sit. Unless we're right there beside someone, it's hard to see from their perspective. And if we are next to that person, it's time to ease their burden with some practical help, instead of condemnation. Indeed, being able to share another's burden of despair or weariness can change their outcome—and that can make a big difference to all the Judys.

Judy's family chose to care for her at home for a long time. When she finally needed professional care, they fought to get her the best available, and they visited her often. Their loving choice meant Judy was able to share her smile far and wide, and that she could leave us with the enduring, and endearing, memory of her dancing. And who can tell how many people's lives were improved by that?

DEVELOPING VIRTUES

A community service club held a bottle drive fundraiser to provide impoverished neighbours with shelter, food, clothing, medical supplies, winter fuel, and other simple necessities of life. Residents saved their returnable bottles and cans for months, and placed them outdoors one Friday night so teams of volunteers could collect them the next morning. Before daybreak, a handful of individuals toured the neighbourhood and collected the recyclables for themselves. The service club arrived a couple of hours later to find everything gone.

This had happened before in the fundraiser's history, on a lesser scale. The community had shrugged its collective shoulders and concluded that the thieves must have needed the money. This time, however, the thieves were people who had already benefited from the service club's generosity, and were stealing from themselves and from others in similar situations. The outrage was palpable, and some volunteers treated the confessed culprits to an old-fashioned verbal dressing-down. Comments flew about the stupidity of people who bite the hand that feeds them. Folks shook their heads in sadness, concluding that the culprits likely didn't know any better. They had no sense of right and wrong. They had no moral character. They didn't understand how to be good because no one had ever taught them.

It was interesting that people decided goodness needed to be taught, because for many years it seems we've expected people to learn goodness by absorption. But in a culture that expects nice guys to finish last, and where finishing first is of utmost importance, a good and virtuous life has become seriously unattractive. Churches may preach virtue, youth groups may reward positive behaviour, and service clubs may vigorously practice helping your neighbour, but member numbers are diminishing. Are we in danger of becoming a culture of self-centred bums? Is it too late for us to learn to be good?

Not according to a Canadian program founded almost twenty-five years ago to promote the virtues of being virtuous. The Virtues Project was established by Linda Kavelin-Popov, her husband, Dr. Dan Popov, and brother John Kavelin after a tea-table discussion in Victoria, BC, about rising levels of violence. The trio deduced that every world religion and belief system holds the same essential positive traits that we call virtues, traits that are being lost. The program lists love, kindness, justice, diligence, service, compassion, humility, friendliness, excellence, tolerance, honesty, strength, generosity, and patience as just some of the fifty-one human characteristics that reduce violence and crime, improve mental health, and promote caring communities.

To help restore these virtues, the group compiled a Virtues Guide for families, and soon found themselves giving workshops on how to teach virtues to children, parents, educators, and community leaders. Initially they were invited by First Nations communities, but the program soon spread worldwide. The Virtues Project has been recognized by the United Nations, used as a business training tool, adopted as a national anti-crime strategy, included in school anti-bullying protocols, and become ingrained in every aspect of daily life for many.

Imagine a world where humility had greater cachet than flamboyant selfishness, or if we were encouraged to try harder instead of just letting go, or shouldered responsibility instead of passing the buck and the blame. Imagine how our communities would look if a trait like helpfulness were valued more than helping ourselves. Imagine the difference it might make to a small community's little bottle drive, itself an event attempting to make a difference. Imagine the effect on our world if we each focused on just one virtue a day for a year? We can do that.

VOCATION

Here's a joke that made me think. Originally it was one of those long, tedious stories that make people roll their eyes and scroll quickly to the end of the email. So this is the abbreviated version.

A duck walks into a pub, orders a beer and a sandwich, and, to the natural surprise of the bartender, sits down to read the newspaper. As well as being a walking, talking, beer-drinking, sandwich-eating, newspaper-reading bird, this duck is also quite sarcastic when the bartender notices that his customer has feathers and webbed feet. Over lunch, the duck confides to the amazed barkeep that he's a drywaller working at a nearby construction site.

Every day for the next two weeks the duck lunches at the pub. When the circus comes to town, the ringmaster patronizes the same pub. The bartender falls over himself with excitement telling the ringmaster all about the amazing duck, and suggests the bird would make a wonderful addition to the circus. The ringmaster asks the bartender to pass the duck his business card.

The bartender complies, and tells the duck he's lined up a new high-paying job for him at the circus. The duck wants to know if this is a circus in a tent made of canvas, with steel cages for the animals, and trailers where the performers live. "Yup," says the barman.

"So," asks the duck, "what do they want with a drywaller?"

Deconstructing the story a bit, it's funny. First, because walking, talking, beer-guzzling, drywalling ducks do not exist. Secondly, the duck's response to the job offer is unexpected. In our minds, a humanized duck belongs in a circus, not at a construction site, so the duck's single-minded pursuit of his drywalling career surprises us. And the duck notices a point we miss: there's probably not a square metre of drywall anywhere in a circus operation. (Then there's the quasi-subtle hint that good drywallers are as scarce as talking ducks.) But the part that made me think is that the duck knows his vocation. He's a drywaller; a feathered, quacking, waddling, web-footed duck of a drywaller, and that's that. It doesn't matter what everyone else thinks, because this is one brave, self-confident duck.

Real drywallers may also be good singers or artists. They may excel at baseball, track and field, maths, or parsing sentences. Their skin may a different colour from ours, or they may speak a language we don't understand. They may be tall, smart, the life of the party, funny, good-looking, or none of the above. But if they are drywallers, or anything else, it's not our job to judge them suitable for a circus sideshow. Of course, the same is true for electricians, nurses, atomic engineers, teachers, writers, mechanics, parents, sailors, farmers, clowns…you name it. We are who we are. We can, and should, change and grow throughout our lives, just as that duck might someday decide to switch careers. But while our roles may change, each one of us has unique gifts and skills that give us a place in the world. Paraphrasing from a letter or two St. Paul wrote a couple of thousand years ago, we are not all called to do the same thing, and we all have different gifts that help us fulfil whatever role we accept in life.

A world full of nothing but talking ducks would not function well, nor would one full of drywallers, bartenders, or ringmasters. We are like pieces of a jigsaw puzzle, where all the little bits, all different colours and shapes, fit together to form a harmonious whole. The harmony is lost when pieces are forced or bent into position just so we can finish the picture in a hurry. Like the duck, we need to find where we fit. Who knows, we may even belong in the circus.

EVERY DAY'S A NEW DAY

In the movie *As Good As It Gets*, Jack Nicholson's character tells his love interest, played by Helen Hunt, that he
wants to be a better man because of her. For him, that means
taking his prescribed meds and being slightly more generous and tolerant, even if it is for mostly selfish reasons. This
simple strategy wins him the hand of the lady. We all want
to be better people, rather than worse, but how do we define
that? Our expectations for ourselves run the gamut from regular teeth-brushing to sainthood. However, we tend to pick
a single aspect of our lives at a time for our self-improvement
schemes, despite being whole people with coexisting physical, emotional, and spiritual needs.

A specific focus on our physicality may lead to a vow to
quit unhealthy habits, lose weight, join a gym, or become
an NHL first-round pick. Emotionally, we might promise
to think one cheerful thought each day, tell someone "I
love you," or to simply avoid situations that make us angry.
Spiritual goals may include daily meditation, studying holy
literature, or following religious teachings more closely.
Sometimes we accomplish these compartmentalized goals,
and sometimes we don't. When we don't, it could be that
we expect too much in the time frame we allot ourselves, or
because other aspects of our lives get in the way of our commitment to our stated goals. Then we beat ourselves up and
give up, or we try again, and again.

At each new beginning we like to make resolutions. At
the beginning of a relationship, we vow to be faithful and

loving. At a journey's beginning, we promise to be patient and observe the rules of the road. Every Monday we vow that this week we'll stick to our promises. In September we tell ourselves we'll do all our homework on time, and on January 1st we promise to quit smoking or lose weight. But a lifetime, a year, a semester, or even a week is a long stretch to stick to a resolution to be a better person. Depending on the state of our personal disrepair, sometimes all we can manage is a day or even an hour at a time, just putting one foot in front of the other. So it was a delight for me to stumble across something called "A Morning Resolve" during an online search for an entirely unrelated subject. No author was cited, but it's from the US-based Forward Movement's website, and it goes like this:

> I will try this day to live a simple, sincere and serene life, repelling promptly every thought of discontent, anxiety, discouragement, impurity, and self-seeking; cultivating cheerfulness, magnanimity, charity, and the habit of holy silence; exercising economy in expenditure, generosity in giving, carefulness in conversation, diligence in appointed service, fidelity to every trust, and a childlike faith in God.
>
> In particular I will try to be faithful in those habits of prayer, work, study, physical exercise, eating, and sleep which I believe the Holy Spirit has shown me to be right.

It covers just about everything, and it's a tall order—almost scary. But it goes on to remind us that in our personal weakness, we can depend on our Creator's comforting strength to support us in our quest for self-improvement. And, see? It says, "I will try *this* day…" That's a new start every day—the first day in the rest of a life.

GIVING

Alot of people in this country work for nothing, but that does not mean they are worth nothing. They are, themselves, gifts to God.

We need our volunteers. Their work, and that of non-profit organizations, eases the financial burden on the public purse. The government runs no soup kitchens or food banks; it mostly leaves the operations of women's refuges, men's support groups, homeless shelters, and children's clubs to the volunteer and private sectors. A lot of museums, school trips, fire brigades, community events, and hospital equipment would not exist without the not-for-profit and volunteer sectors. It's real work that needs to be done, not pie-in-the-sky fantasy stuff. And it's done by people who already know how to do it—or learn quickly, from necessity.

Oh, it's true that various levels of government shell out money (ours) to various organizations and facilities associated with each of the aforementioned endeavours, but only if they are already government programs—or they fight tooth and nail for funding. Competition for the public dollar is intense, and often requires that applicants toil for days filling out forms and trying to read the fickle minds of the folks controlling the purse strings. Meanwhile, money and attention seem to flow fairly easily towards big business or big government, as if they need it more.

Sometimes they do. But having witnessed first-hand the largesse and waste in commerce and government, it would be hard to persuade me that they can't find the funds or energy they need lurking somewhere within their organizations. On the other hand, charities and not-for-profit organizations work on tight budgets, and the tiniest cuts can kill. Yet these organizations survive, which demonstrates that the people operating not-for-profit organizations have skills that must outstrip those of any begging fat cat corporation. Or maybe it's because they commit to their goals, not to their paycheques.

Volunteers may have minimal education, but the same goes for highly paid employees of government and big business. They may live in small communities, but so do multi-millionaires. They may be willing to carry out menial jobs, but there are no small jobs, only small people. They may be highly educated with the potential to run the world, but choose to help others instead of helping themselves. They may live in cities, but maintain a small-town neighbourliness. They may be leaders in their organizations, where each task and every person who does them are important to achieving a goal.

Judging others by the work they do is as wrong as judging them by their skin colour, their gender, or the way they speak. We are all guilty of making these kinds of judgments. We assume that scuffed clothing means a dull mind. We assume that a first name embroidered on a uniform demonstrates a lesser impact on society than a brass nameplate on a polished desk. Reverse snobbery also exists: we assume that someone with shiny shoes can't possibly know how to hammer a nail, or that a university graduate is probably an impractical daydreamer.

Baloney.

Such clues may help us sort out the people we meet every day, but first impressions are often incorrect. Allowing those impressions to influence future interactions with the same people is just wrong. We can all work on correcting that mistake. What's holding us back?

ACCIDENTAL GIFTS

When Viola Desmond sat in New Glasgow's Roseland Theatre back in 1946, the foremost thing on her mind was filling in time while waiting for a garage to repair her car so she could continue her trip to Sydney. Instead, the tiny woman was dragged out of the theatre and thrown in jail. After sitting sternly all night in the town lock-up, Viola Desmond was convicted the next morning of a penny's worth of tax evasion. It was her first time at the theatre, and she sat in a slightly more expensive main-floor seat instead of a cheaper seat in the balcony, for which she had paid.

That was the cover story. The real story was that the theatre's main floor was only for white people and Viola Desmond was of African ancestry. The real story was racism. The incident is a gross blemish on Canadian legal, social, and cultural history.

Viola Desmond fought the conviction, and lost. The stress of the ordeal led to the breakup of her marriage and destroyed her health. She gave up a promising business career. She died young. She was one small person, in small-town Canada, who stood up against the prevailing ideals of her time, who gave up what she had to fight underhanded racism masquerading as justice. She lost—but she won, for all of us. Racism and prejudice haven't disappeared, and they probably won't, so long as humanity fears diversity. But thanks to Viola Desmond's unplanned sacrifice, we know these things are wrong.

When the Leese family built some tracks into their back-country Nova Scotia woodlot and dug a pond, they simply intended to create an accessible space where disabled family members and friends could fish and enjoy the great outdoors, blackflies and all. It turned out, almost accidentally, that the family donated their property and their daily lives to providing outdoor recreation for thousands of worthy strangers. Lansdowne Outdoor Recreational Development Association creates opportunities for people whose active lives have become restricted by age or disability. LORDA may not have ended all the struggles of seniors or disabled persons, but thanks to the Leeses' labour of love we have hope for the future.

Viola Desmond and the Leeses are not the only people who sacrifice themselves to service. At the most basic level, parents give up much of their own young lives to raise their children. Employees in all walks of life go above and beyond the call of paid duty to ensure completion of projects or programs that will make a positive difference in the world. Ordinary people commit extraordinary service, and the rest of us often don't even notice. They meet their challenges with courage, love, compassion, and a healthy measure of stubbornness. When they sacrifice, we all win.

The theme of Christianity is service, sacrifice, and triumph; losing one's self, but winning more for eternity. But there are many ways to lay down one's love other than dying. It likely didn't occur to Viola Desmond, the Leese family, or any others who give of themselves until it hurts, to follow Jesus's example, or to set an example for others. For them it's not a choice: they do what they have to do. The choice lies with those of us who watch.

FORGIVENESS

On July 12, 1995, Ralph Parker's car struck and killed Renee Lee and Danielle Orichefsky, aged fifteen and thirteen, and injured two other boys, while they stood at a Dartmouth bus stop. Parker was sentenced to two years house arrest for dangerous driving. At a memorial service for his daughters ten years later, Joseph Orichefsky stood in front of 250 people to publicly forgive Parker. Parker tearfully apologized, and the Orichefsky family embraced him. No matter how often we see that kind of spiritual generosity and courage, it still wows us. We were similarly awed when Rev. Dale Lang publicly forgave the youngster who shot his son Jason, in Taber, Alberta, in 1999.

In a world where people can get punched or shot for a minor insult, it's rare and surprising to see forgiveness of a heinous injury or crime. In more than twenty years of newspaper reporting, I have witnessed only two other instances of victims or their families offering their hands or hugs to attackers and killers. Both occasions aroused in me tremendous respect for the grieving and injured parties who were able to offer forgiveness. It was incredible. If I hadn't seen it with my own eyes, I wouldn't believe it.

It's hard to imagine having the same kind of strength in a similar situation. Yet the religions of the world urge forgiveness—it's right up there with loving your neighbour and treating others the way you want to be treated. How many times do Christians mutter to God to "forgive us our trespasses, as we forgive those who trespass against us"? And if we believe God will forgive us, as we are taught, how can we not forgive others? Do we think we are better than God, that we have the power to withhold forgiveness? If we wrong someone else—and we all do—wouldn't we want that person to forgive us?

Most of us consider ourselves to be pretty good citizens. We don't set out every morning with the intention of hurting others, we try to be courteous and thoughtful of others, and we donate our time and resources to a host of charities and causes. That's difficult enough at times, but never so hard as forgiving those who have grieved us. It is a sign of maturity not to bite back when we are bitten, like toddlers in a sandbox. But as we age, our petty vengeance takes other forms. We may refuse to speak to a relative who said something we didn't like at last year's family picnic, or spout off at the clerk who sold us a deficient toaster—as if it were his fault—or strike the person who just ran into our back bumper.

In these examples, we aren't seeking justice—an event that may, or may not, be necessary to forgiveness. Instead we're seeking revenge, a meal that is best served cold. Imagine how much better the world would be if, when we were hurt, we took a deep breath and waited until we settled down before acting. It could take hours, days, or years to consider the source of the hurt and the potential damage of vengeance, to place the injury in perspective and plan to move on.

By most standards, if anyone had reason to be angry and revengeful it would be the Orichefsky and Lang families. Legal justice has been meted out in both cases, but the loss of family members hurts long after the expiration of court-ordered penalties. Rather than revenge, however, these two families sought healing through forgiveness. The rest of us can only hope and pray we never find out how hard that is. But for practice, just in case we ever need to know, we can try to follow their example as we face the small hurts of everyday life. It's a gift to a hurting world.

GOODNESS

There was once a little boy whose family, through no fault of their own, faced a crisis. At the tender age of four, the boy decided that he really couldn't help because the situation was out of his control. But he figured that he could make his family's life easier by being a "good boy." He didn't consider being a firefighter, hockey star, or astronaut; he would just be good. For him, that meant listening to the grown-ups in charge when it came to tidying his toys, picking up his clothes, and taking his dishes to the sink. He watched his mom and dad closely, and if they needed something he trotted off to fetch it before being asked. He fed the pets and was kind to his siblings. He went to bed on time and came to the supper table when called. He was a dependable, responsible child who smiled often. He tried really hard to do nothing that would upset anyone else, and he mostly succeeded.

At first it was hard for the boy to always think of the right thing to do, but it got easier with time and he got used to "being good." The habit of helpfulness stayed with him even into his teen years, when his personal rebellion featured weird clothes and music, unusually daring athletic pursuits, and building strange furniture from junk. He was popular and enjoyed average grades in school. His parents were proud of him. They were confident he would do the right thing—but, like most parents, they weren't always right. The boy sometimes lost his temper and made stupid choices, but mostly he was still good.

Then, as a young man, he discovered first-hand that bad things can happen to good people. He succumbed to his hurt and despair and spiralled into the isolation of substance abuse. But old habits die hard. Even at his lowest, he continued to clean up after himself and care about others. With time, his goodness asserted itself and he recovered. Today he is an upstanding citizen and a loving, patient husband and father, in a career that helps countless others survive their crises just as his family did. He has made a positive difference in his family, among his friends, and in the next generation, all because he decided a long time ago to be a good boy.

Without knowing that he had made a conscious decision to "be good," or how easy it would have been to choose another road, some might say that little boy was destined to grow into the man he became. But when he resolved to be good, it meant choosing to do good things. The difference between good and bad may seem more obvious to a child than to world-weary grown-ups. For children, good and bad are opposites with no shades of grey, so if one thing is good, the other choice could be perceived as bad. By the time he became an adult, the boy had trained himself in the basics of being good, so more complicated dilemmas were easier to solve.

Every new year, my own resolutions are in danger of following the dodo into extinction. But if that little boy could stick with his resolution until it became habit, then anyone can. We can each decide to be good, wherever we are. Consider it a pebble tossed into the pond of humanity, sending positive ripples throughout the world. Consider it our gift to a world needing goodness.

SAINTS UNDER CONSTRUCTION

Brother André did windows. A thin, frail man, he also washed floors, lugged firewood, carried messages, and cleaned oil lamps at the Quebec college where he worked for forty years. On October 17, 2010, seventy-three years after he died, the Roman Catholic Church canonized Brother André as a saint. There's probably a long and inspiring story about how Alfred Bessette, one of ten orphaned children from a nineteenth-century working-class family, gained worldwide respect for the healing miracles that happened in his presence; whose fame for nursing sick people back to good health through prayer when all else had failed caused lineups at the college. He was also largely responsible for the construction of St. Joseph's Oratory, a Montreal centre of miraculous healing that he credited to St. Joseph.

But for me, it's the fact that Saint André, as he's now known, washed windows.

Brother André knew what it was like to have chilly, dirty water run down his arms and into his clothing as he scrubbed sooty grime from the panes at Notre Dame College in Montreal. He also knew how sore one's knees and back can get while crawling across a floor to lift the muddy footprints of others. He would have borne the frustration and anger of those to whom he delivered unwanted or disturbing news. He likely got sawdust in his eyes and tripped over the doorstep while carrying logs from the woodpile to the stove. And it's a safe bet that over his career he swept up the broken glass from a few shattered lamp chimneys. Menial labour did not diminish the soul of this man. On the other hand, André wasn't sainted simply because of his hard physical labour, but for his deep faith and healing miracles. There's got to be a lesson in there somewhere.

Rightly or wrongly, society believes that prominent wealthy people are more likely to be selfish sinners and poor people noble saints. A comparison of two Canadians, the saint André (Alfred) Bessette and the wealthy serial murderer Colonel Russell Williams, might support the statement that it's hard for a rich person to get into heaven. It's easier to admire the good spiritual health of a financially challenged person than it is to applaud the good works of someone who enjoys every material advantage. But poverty is not a prerequisite for goodness, nor is wealth a precondition for evil. We can't measure our worth with money. Nor can we say that a particular job automatically equals poverty of the wallet or the soul.

Our jobs become our identities. We invest education, time, and energy into doing them well and we work hard to rise in our chosen fields, whatever they may be. We find out just how important our jobs are when we lose them, but losing a job should never mean losing ourselves. We are bigger than our jobs. What we do is important, but how we do it is even more important. Cheerfulness, honesty, humility, generosity, care, dedication, and charity are as important in a fish-gutter as they are in the head of the consortium that owns the fish plant.

We can't fake those attributes, even to attract business. Angry, dishonest, conceited, mean, lazy, and hate-filled people are soon found out, regardless of their disguise. Sadly for them, they are often avoided and rarely remembered with joy. Building our careers should not mean we ignore our souls, any more than spiritual health care means forgetting our vocations. Brother André proved it: saints under construction can still do windows.

ALL THINGS ARE POSSIBLE

The teacher drew a straight line on the chalkboard, about the length of his forearm. "That line," he said, "goes on forever."

My whole grade-four class swivelled to look from one side of the room to the other and chorused, "No it doesn't."

"Use your imaginations," the teacher instructed. He went on to explain that he could keep going with the chalk until it wore out, then continue with another piece, and another piece, and another. He could keep drawing that line forever. Never mind that the line was straight, more or less, and the Earth is round, or that he'd have died long before "forever" arrived. Theoretically, he said, he could never draw the end of that line. It would go on and on into infinity, into the furthermost parts of the universe and beyond—if there was a beyond. This was my introduction to geometry, to the concept of infinity, and, I suppose, to the notion that a weird idea might actually make sense to me if I thought about it long enough and hard enough.

That teacher was a brave man to spring such a concept on a bunch of wide-eyed nine-year-olds. Picture us going home to explain it to our parents, wondering if we would somehow trip over all those lines intersecting all over the place. But children are good at believing, because they have fertile imaginations and haven't yet been taught to think that some things can't be done. To them, nothing is impossible. Kids have no problem understanding that a fat man in a red suit, carrying enough gifts for all the children in the world, can squeeze through a seven-inch flue. Rabbits laying eggs and fairies carting away bags of discarded teeth—why not?

What if monkeys could talk? (Maybe they can.) What if I could fly past the sun? (Could happen.) What if I invented something that could save the world? (I might.) What if there were something big in the sky that would look after me—or something evil under the bed that would grab my feet in the dark? (You never know.) But by the time we become adults, we have sorted through all the what-ifs, the dreams, and the fantasies. We come up with our personal lists of priorities, possibilities, and goals, and we set out to achieve them.

It's too bad our lists don't usually include that line that stretches to infinity, but instead focus on getting along, on survival. We are so busy simply putting one foot in front of the other that most of the time our minds don't push the boundaries of here and now. It's not that we adults are incapable of believing in the odd or unproven. There are many of us who conscientiously avoid stepping on cracks in the sidewalk, who must leave a house by the same door we enter, refuse to take an old broom to a new home, or count crows for joy or sorrow.

Scientific proof or not, a lot of people believe in Jesus's resurrection, Groundhog Day predictions, angels, the power of crystals or pyramids, ghosts, the benefits or disadvantages of certain foods, and/or extraterrestrial beings. They are the people who say, "Why not?" instead of "Absolutely not."

Some call those beliefs superstitions, and say we are too intelligent to accept those ideas. We don't believe in anything that can't be seen, heard, touched, tasted, or smelled. If it cannot be proven, then it cannot be true. But is anyone alive on Earth today really smart enough to know with absolute certainty what is fact and what is superstition? Wouldn't that be an assumption? How could we know for sure?

History shows us that once upon a time only weirdos went out on a limb to declare the Earth was round, that it revolved around the sun. The weirdos won; the skeptics lost. We don't know the limits of creation, and we don't know where the line ends. Just imagine how much more there is to discover.

PART VI

Believe

GOD GAVE US BRAINS
FOR THINKING

It's easier to believe what we are told than to discover things for ourselves. When it comes to research, or study, or even a stroll down the street to see what all the commotion is about, we would rather wait to read about it in the paper. If information is filtered through someone else's eyes and then handed to us on a page or a screen, we tend to believe it even if our own experience tells us otherwise. My favourite example of this involves a man who attended a marathon. He saw with his own eyes who won. He heard the cheers of the crowd and spoke with the winner afterwards. But when a news agency mistakenly reported that another person had won, he passed on the information as if it were true, and ignored the evidence of his own eyes and ears.

As a species, we humans are lazy thinkers, and maybe becoming more so. We accept any old pap that's fed to our trusting little minds and then, when we discover we've been fed a load of hogwash, we blame the person or organization who fed it to us. The more a situation demands of our intellect, the more we depend on others to interpret that situation for us. We want the executive summaries of research papers, the distilled reports of budget details, and simple instructions for our appliances. When none of that is available, we throw up our hands and tell ourselves it just doesn't matter. At that point we simply repeat warnings that everything we do causes cancer, that the folks in charge are conspiring against us, or that you need to be a rocket scientist to set up the DVD player.

It's just too hard to study a subject and draw our own conclusions, to work through the figures on a balance sheet so we can understand where the money really went, or to learn the names of all the little holes in the backs, bellies, and sides of electronic equipment. It is true that life would be terribly complicated if we insisted on personally experiencing every drop of the great swamp of knowledge that exists on the planet today. There are, however, issues that we can't leave to someone else to experience and translate for us.

Love is one of those.

If our expectations of love depend on books, television, radio, video games, or internet fantasies, then we won't know love when it jumps up and bites us while we're sitting on our balconies waiting for the cartoon prince to rescue us from drudgery. As if! If our understanding of hope comes from exactly following the directions of a chain letter so that we will experience good luck in five days, or following a certain sequence of activities so as not to offend a real or imagined spirit, then we live in dread, not firm anticipation. If our faith consistently and entirely depends on others telling us what to believe, there will come a time when it's challenged and it falls apart like wet tissue paper.

Spiritual or religious faith begs to be challenged in order to survive. We just cannot take someone else's word that there is a God, and God does this or that, and in order to be good with God we must say these words and bend that way and sit in this part of a particular building on a particular day, and then state that we have faith. It's not sensible. Certainly we can believe as children do, innocently, freshly, and openly. But, think about it: who asks more questions than children? If we accept a belief system just because we've been told it's good for us, or spurn a faith just because we've been told not to believe it, or deny religion because we rebel against a childhood of being told to believe, we are more childish than child-like. We need to question our own individual beliefs in order to get a handle on them. It's hard to know what to believe until we study what there is to believe, and why other people believe what they do. It's not a journey for the lazy, and no one else can truly do it for us.

It's an odd thing that faith is such an individual journey, yet it requires interaction with others and with all of creation in order to develop. It appears as if we are wired for personal spirituality, and also to enjoy the miracle of community. So while finding faith may not be for wimps, we're not in it alone.

EXISTENCE

My toy rocket got lost in the woods here last week. It shot high in the sky until it almost disappeared. Then streamers popped out and the rocket sailed downward to some obscure spot behind a stand of poplar and larch. Searching the damp undergrowth aroused plenty of mosquitoes, but the bright yellow-and-blue-finned cardboard tube remained invisible despite its long orange streamers. It's there, though, because grade-school science taught me that everything has to be somewhere, and so far nothing has persuaded me otherwise. My toy rocket does exist. I heard it, saw it, felt it, and even smelled the scorched launch pad. It remains lost simply because I've looked in all the wrong places.

The little rocket is like so many things we seek in life: things we can reach out and touch, like a car that doesn't need maintenance every two weeks, a house that holds all our junk, or sneakers that really fit. They're out there, they exist, but we just don't have them. Then there are the goals we can't measure, things like love, happiness, success, acceptance, security, and satisfaction. Add to that list the need to feel we are part of something bigger than ourselves, something more powerful, something greater than the sum of humanity + universe.

Today's plethora of New Age spirituality and rejigged ancient theologies demonstrates a yearning for something above and beyond our puny human understanding. We humans seek somewhere or someone to visit in our hearts and minds, something holy and life-giving that can bless us as we wish to be blessed. We want a place to pour out our damaged selves and be refilled by something better and more encouraging than we can imagine.

Traditionalists belonging to one religion or another name this entity God, manitou, Kesoo'lkw, Allah, Author, Lord, Almighty, Christ, Creator, and at least as many other words as there are languages. We are confident in our particular spiritual interpretations and don't care what anyone else thinks of our faith. We are absolutely sure of our beliefs, and often offensively smug in that certainty. We know where the rocket sits, and we'll walk you right to it—once we persuade you to wade through swamps and thickets of thorns filled with fire-breathing alligators.

One the other end of the spectrum, scoffers say no deity exists, that everything we have and are comes from us, and what we accomplish—within, of course, the bounds of the sensible god: Science. The rocket is gone, it's never coming back—and what were we thinking, playing with rockets in the first place?

In between sit the seekers. Traditional organized religions with their rules, petty politics, and contradictory doctrines cause dismay and confusion that cloud their true meanings. But seekers know there is a rocket (or parts of a rocket) out there, if only we can find it. We'll sing, dance, beat drums, consult oracles, turn over cards, light candles, watch the sky, ingest unusual substances, invent myths…we will do almost everything imaginable to satisfy our need for communion with the great soul of the universe. We're the ones running frantically in all directions trying to find that rocket, trying this way and that path until we sit, exhausted, lost, and empty. Then suddenly: *boing!* The rocket falls from a tree and hits us on the head. When that happens, we carry it with us, out of the wilderness.

BONES OF BELIEF

A tempest raged among theologians, archaeologists, and historians over the scholarship—or lack thereof—behind a 2007 television documentary that claimed bones discovered in Jerusalem were those of Jesus and his wife and kids. The controversy attracted the attention of people who don't normally bother with the whys and wherefores of faith, Christian or otherwise. At the very least, it made people think. For non-Christians, the dust-up tweaked some vague curiosity and interest in another religious system. For non-believers, it was additional proof that religion creates fools who will argue over anything. Ordinary Christians in pews wondered what the fuss was about.

Christians are the ones who buy into the concept that one version of God's three persons was born to a mortal mother in a barn, and worshipped by neighbourhood shepherds who heard about the baby from a bunch of angels singing in the sky. Rich, foreign scholars followed a star to find the child, bringing him expensive presents. The baby's growth to manhood was so low profile it was almost invisible, but all of a sudden, some thirty years later, Jesus burst onto the public scene. For three years his speeches and miraculous acts attracted a lot of attention, good and bad; religious and community leaders saw him as a threat to the society of the day, and he was tortured and killed. Three days later he rose from the dead, body and all, and walked around and visited people. He later ascended into heaven, but his spirit came back to live inside everyone who believes.

As stories go, it's a pretty amazing one—especially if you haven't heard it from childhood and therefore become accustomed to it. So the discovery of Jesus's tomb is one more fantastic story, apparently backed up by smart, educated people who can name places, dates, and people. Jesus's body couldn't have risen from the dead and left his bones behind, so positively identifying a first-century skeleton as his interferes with the Easter story of resurrection, which is central to Christianity. But the show's detractors say the problem is not with the documentary's effect on Christian faith, but that it was inadequately researched, unscientific, non-historic bunk passed off as truth.

Similar controversies surrounded Mel Gibson's *The Passion of the Christ*, Dan Brown's *The DaVinci Code*, and the Shroud of Turin investigations, just to name a few. Observers argue over presentation, historical accuracy, and points of view. History shoots plot lines out of the firmament, political correctness subverts history, and truth gets sanitized to the point of being cute.

It probably comes as a surprise to many that religion could possibly be based on history and science, because faith is so dependent on just that, faith. People believe what they believe because they believe it. When it comes down to the choice between belief and disbelief, proof is unnecessary. Even the belief that there is no God is still a belief, if any evidence to the contrary leaves the believer unmoved. Asked to explain the wonder of the universe or factual accounts of mysterious and miraculous events, either now or in ages past, atheists will attribute them to the natural progression of the world: science. The rest of the world will credit God, by whatever name we know him or her. But they won't discount science, as demonstrated by the persistent investigations into the histories of the world's various faiths.

Just a little research can show that places and dates and people in Bible stories really existed. It would be silly to assume otherwise, given that we can prove dinosaurs once walked the planet millions of years before old Father Abraham. If we can prove fantastical creatures once existed, why not a well-documented historical leader?

The tools of science—carbon dating, DNA analysis, global positioning systems—are trained on the question, What is the nature of God?

Maybe someday science will prove what so many already believe.

THE RETURN FROM ROCK BOTTOM

When we hit rock bottom, there are those of us who claw our way up with our nails and our teeth, and those who scream for a ladder. But the only way out from down is up.

The bottom of the well of despair, poverty, addiction, pain, or any other human misery is a dark and lonely place, no matter how many people are down there with you. Most of us have likely felt, at some time in our lives, that if we have to suffer one more second of a particular burden, we'll just die. But one more second does go by, and then two, and then minutes, hours, days, or even years—and we don't die.

Sometimes the situation resolves easily: the dentist finishes drilling, the chicken pox fades away, ten days of rain give way to sunshine, or a big multinational company moves into town and everyone gets a job. Other times the burden becomes heavier, the pain gets worse, and it becomes a sink-or-swim situation. We keep paddling just to stay afloat, but we don't get anywhere, and we become exhausted staying in the same place. Eventually we strike bottom, which is in a different place for everyone.

Past the "Why me?" point and the "I'm a nasty person and I must have done something bad to deserve this" stages is "I can't do this anymore." Even if you've never been to that place before, you'll recognize it when you get there. It's when the human spirit gives up and calls out for divine intervention. It's when there is nothing more we can do to improve things, and it's all up to someone else who is bigger and better and stronger.

Reaching the end of our rope is such a universal human experience that it's described in poetry and prose—and in clichés. (Just count them in the preceding sentences!) But when it's happening to you, it doesn't feel like a romantic tragedy, a pretty poster in a teen's room, a sweet saying on a bookmark, or a piece of advice passed around in an email chain letter. Being told that *Every path has a few puddles*, or *If God brings you to it, he will bring you through it*, doesn't make us feel better when we're looking up that long, dark tunnel toward a dim and distant light.

Our inability to heed such advice, even when it's trite and light, must be part of the human condition. It's as if we must bounce off that wall before we can change direction, like a wind-up toy car. For some reason, we refuse to benefit from others' experience and wisdom. We have to find out for ourselves. We have to learn the hard way. Given our stubbornness, it's amazing that anyone ever returns from the bottom, but time and again, we do.

Some of us have to go bankrupt before we learn how to handle our personal resources. We may be at death's door before we can kick a chemical addiction. We may be shunned by friends and associates before we realize our own pathological greed or anger. When bitterness sets in following an unpreventable illness or injury, we may let it rot our souls until there's nothing left to sustain our bodies.

We all know folks whose life situation is so hard we could reasonably expect them to be cranky and fearful and bitter, but instead they are kind and hopeful and sweet. The people I know who are like that have been to the wall. They have sat in the darkness at the bottom of the well, and looked up. Their journey back was a rocky road, and they admit they didn't—couldn't—do it alone. They called on their god, and they were not afraid to welcome the support of their community.

I once heard a sermon exhorting us to pray with the urgency of one being forcibly held under water. When you hit rock bottom, that's what you do. And if we are not in an urgent situation ourselves, it doesn't hurt to pray for someone else who is. God knows there are enough of them.

THERE IS A TOMORROW

After almost two decades of gathering news from northern Nova Scotia, the town of Trenton became synonymous in my mind with *The Little Engine That Could*. For anyone who doesn't know the famous children's story, it's about a little steam locomotive hauling a huge load, trying to climb a mighty hill. The little train tells itself (it talks, of course—this *is* a children's story!) that it can make it to the top of the hill. Chanting in time to the steam-driven wheels, it says, "I think I can, I think I can, I think I can." And in spite of all those who say it can't be done and refuse to try it for themselves, the little engine is successful. Over the peak, on the faster downhill track, it puffs triumphantly, "I thought I could, I thought I could, I thought I could." The story's message to children (and everyone else) is to believe in yourself even when no one else does.

The Little Engine analogy likely came to my mind because, until the railcar plant closed for good in 2007, trains were produced in Trenton, Nova Scotia. Add to that the town's numerous layoffs and other economic disappointments. Then marvel at how its people still consider their cups half full, and believe they can conquer the highest mountains hauling whatever baggage they have. There are many reasons for despair, but like many Atlantic Canadian towns this community has a culture of optimism.

Trenton is not the only economically beleaguered community in the region, hammered by waves of unemployment, unfortunate economics, or unfriendly policies. Nor is it the only town with dreams of growth and prosperity. Visit any similar-sized community in Nova Scotia and you'll find strategic plans, consultants' reports, and economic proposals, all aimed at improving citizens' prospects. Green spaces, business parks, and communal lots are installed for the use and enjoyment of future population growth. Residents look firmly forward—even if, logically, the future seems as bleak as a beach in April. But optimism is not about logic, it's about spirit, and not just community spirit or pride in the place we each call home. Just about every village on earth is home to people who believe they live in the best place on the planet, and who would move heaven and earth to stay there and live happily ever after.

There is probably no proper term for the kind of spirit that keeps communities rowing hard forward while their stern fills with water, but maybe it's closer to determination than it is to pride. We are certain that if we keep bailing and rowing, we'll make it. People work hard to save a community when it looks like it's about to founder, because history tells them it's been done before, so it can probably be done again. Some of the oldest communities on the continent are in Nova Scotia, frequent victims of the boom-and-bust cycle. They teach us that we can pull ourselves up by our bootstraps and change our destinies, but not by sitting on our hands.

We have learned that sometimes we have to start over. We have learned that when the coal, the gold, the lumber, and the fish are all gone, we still have ourselves. We have learned that there is more than one way to make a living. We have learned that when one door closes, another opens—and we're not afraid to stick our heads through and holler.

The Little Engine That Could doesn't tell us what happens to the little locomotive after its big achievement. Does it bust a boiler? Burn out its firebox? Is it ever able to climb another mountain? And why did the little engine think it could do the job? Was it experience? Was it a realistic assessment of its own strength? The trick in getting over the mountain is not just in simply thinking that we can do it. The trick is knowing that we have what it takes, recognizing and accepting the consequences, and then doing it.

It's faith.

COINCIDENCE?

It's funny how things happen. During an extremely busy month, populated by isolated little tasks, several ongoing major projects, deadlines, extra responsibilities, and catching up, it seemed like I was buried in work. Then suddenly a forgotten writing job jumped from the page of my daybook with a deadline of that very day. I had only hours to go, no time for research or forethought or meditation, no ideas percolating in my head, and no inspiration. It was time to panic, but checking my email seemed to be a good way to put off screaming and pulling out my hair.

And there it was, like a message from the Almighty: *Relax and reconnect with God.* Actually it was an advertisement for a fifty-cent pamphlet on eliminating stress—but God is perfectly capable of communicating with us via Internet marketing if that's what God wants to do. The pamphlet was written, not by God, of course, but by a human who commiserated with my inability to slow down and asked, *Are you stressed? Do you need a rest?* Stressed? Rest? After just four hours of sleep, three hours of fighting with a recalcitrant computer, and no breakfast, that seemed like a silly question. But it was the perfect reminder at the right time. Relax and reconnect with God.

Connecting with God is a bit like dieting: anyone who's done it before knows how, but we put it off until the moment is right. Then all of a sudden last winter's jacket doesn't fit and we are reminded that it's time to pay attention to what we eat. We could put off talking with God until the perfect moment if we were smart enough to know when that was. But we wait until we get stressed or sad or lost, and then God finds a way to reach out to us—even if it's through an e-advertisement.

Yes, it's true that the ad that landed on my desktop was written and sent by a human, and not by God. It's true that weariness can make one vulnerable to psychological manipulation, and that one can see ghosts in every corner and meaning in the meaningless if one is so inclined. But connecting with God, or experiencing God connecting to us, happens in many different ways. A friend of mine often speaks of fate and how, just when she is in need, that need is filled by someone or something. This knowledge allows her to go through life with confidence in the future, whatever it brings. One man described to me, time and again, how a brief prayer helps him find lost objects. I tried it, and it worked, which surprised me. People have told me how terrible events became life-altering experiences that put them in touch with their god, by whatever name. They've told me how "chance" encounters changed or saved their lives.

Chance? Coincidence? I don't think so.

GOD IS EVERYWHERE

While I was sitting in a bar one day, some people approached me to talk about religion. (You don't often see the words "bar" and "religion" in the same sentence, but that's what happened.) Occasionally people initiate conversations with me about spirituality because they've read my column, or because they are aware of my involvement in a faith community and feel a sense of familiarity. (Also, Nova Scotia is small, so you're bound to meet someone who knows someone you know.)

It's a humbling and almost frightening experience when near-strangers spill their innermost concerns about their faith, the afterlife, their perceptions of and/or disillusionment about religious institutions, and their experiments with alternate spiritual paths. What if I say the wrong thing, or pass off their serious quest for information as a trivial conversation starter? What if this is someone's first trembling step towards expressing personal spirituality and I screw up? How does one provide answers without overwhelming the seeker with preachiness? After all, what do I know? My solution was a quick silent prayer—*God, help me out here*—and more listening than talking. Though I will likely never know the outcome, if any, of our conversation, we ended up sharing laughter and even a few tears as my questioners showed themselves to be intelligent, thoughtful people.

A pint of beer may have made my companions comfortable enough to speak candidly, but it didn't dim their intellect or passion for the subject. Mainline churches yearn to have that kind of urgent interest sitting in their pews. Some religious folks might argue these conversations don't belong in a bar—but why not? Mere humans can't presume to keep the Almighty in a box, constructing rituals and qualifications to restrict access. Jesus taught wherever he was (and notoriously turned water into wine). The Jews had no temple when Moses brought the Ten Commandments from the mountaintop. Muslims may not drink alcohol, but they are called to regular prayer whether in a bar or a bedroom or a mosque. The Buddha found enlightenment under a tree. And on it goes.

Plenty of modern religious leaders take their messages outside the buildings carefully and lovingly constructed as containers of their faith. They use mass media like newspapers, television, radio, and the Internet to spread their message. They hold huge gatherings in gymnasiums and stadiums, testify from street corners or liquor store doorsteps, or call the faithful to worship in shopping centres, airports, or classrooms. Sometimes the fervency of these unconventional leaders makes members of long-established or mainstream religious groups uncomfortable; sometimes they prove to be fakes who disillusion and hurt their followers. However, leaders of mainstream religious groups can also create discomfort, disillusionment, and hurt. Unfortunately, we humans excel at the craft.

We aren't as skilled, though, at the subject of religion. We cling to popular religious myths that tar every believer with a brush coated with hypocrisy and self-service. We also misinterpret faith as perfection and therefore proof of hypocrisy, but it's the other way around: recognizing our imperfections allows us to develop our faith.

My bar encounter was followed that same day by an equally unusual experience. While having supper at a restaurant, a commotion drew my attention to a table surrounded by adolescents, apparently on their way home from a sports tournament. As I watched, they held hands and offered thanks. It was a "wow" kind of day.

God is alive and well, in bars and restaurants and the hearts of folks aplenty.

THE WINDS OF GOD

We can't do anything about which way the wind blows, but we can adjust our sails, says a fridge magnet in my friend's kitchen. Sometimes a good tailwind speeds us on our way; sometimes we battle a strong headwind to get where we want to go; sometimes a storm takes us completely off course; and sometimes a sudden gust bowls us right over. A tail breeze for one person is a headwind for another, so it's not the direction of life's winds, as much as how we adjust our sails, that decides our voyage.

Throughout life, we learn from our experiences and occasionally through advice from others how to adjust our sails. That education doesn't end when we graduate, reach voting age, get married, have our first child, or retire. We learn that life can change in the blink of an eye. A squall comes out of nowhere and our hopes and dreams crash on the rocks. Experiences like sudden illness or injury, fire, job loss, or death of a loved one alter our plans and goals, sometimes permanently. The wind is out of our control, but our response—how we set our sails—is up to us. It's our decision, our choice, but it takes courage and faith to even lift our sails in the first place.

In a 1908 poem Jessie Adams says, "I feel the winds of God today; today my sail I lift." It aptly describes the concept that life's voyage is best done with bravery, based on faith in a Great Pilot that "wilt not let me drift." True story: There was once a man taking sailing lessons who was initially at the head of the class. He caught on quickly to the first instructions. His little sail filled with wind and he scudded across the bay at a wonderful speed, while his classmates fluttered around the instructor like a flock of nervous ducklings around their mama. The would-be sailor had taken off before learning the part about how to turn the boat around, and was headed into the Gulf of St. Lawrence when the instructor took pity and rescued him. The student-sailor chose to let the wind take him, without fear of his lack of skill or experience. He trusted that he would either learn the hard way how to adjust his sails, perish, or be rescued by someone else.

When we decide on a destination, set our sails to get there, and meet strong winds and storms all the way, we can choose to stay the course and stubbornly battle the elements until we reach port, either battered but triumphant or battered and bitter. The risk, of course, is in not making port at all, but life is all about the voyage.

We can also change direction, sometimes dramatically. It might turn out to be the best thing that we ever do, taking us into unplanned, exciting, and profitable waters, or it might bore us to tears. It may be time to test the breeze for the winds of God, and see where they take us.

We can haul in our sails and stay in a safe harbour until conditions improve, confident that we have avoided potential danger and evil, but we can and must put back out to the wide sea. Ships are safe in the harbour, but that's not what ships are for. Renewing our voyage can be difficult after a stormy session. But *we* decide how we want to travel, and how to set our sails. So let the canvas fill and enjoy the ride.

AFTERWORD:
God Goes on Forever

The only constant is change. It has been so since the Greek philosopher Heraclitus first made that pronouncement 2,500 years ago. I would argue that God-the-creator-and-ruler-of-the-universe, by whatever name humans know him or her, also remains constant and unchanging for ever and ever, beyond the end of time. But that's just me, and other people don't necessarily agree. However, we can likely agree that our own lives are changing constantly. And it makes sense that they do: without change there is no life, no growth, and no death.

The world and I have changed in the decade that passed since my *Chronicle Herald* column first appeared in print. The extent of that change became obvious during the editing process for this book, as I adjusted statements to match altered historical circumstances and changed words and phrases to reflect the development of my personal spirituality. The latter came about because the column created a sort of dialogue with readers, who opened my eyes and challenged my viewpoints. Their feedback exhilarated and infuriated me and forced me to grow in my own faith. Some even honoured me by sharing their deepest heartbreaks and their greatest joys, stories which sometimes found their way, anonymously, into later columns.

Uniquely interesting to me were the people who stated their opposition to the concept of a god. Instead, they said they religiously use intelligence, science, innate wisdom, or personal experience to guide their lives—all concepts in which they strongly believe. (Actually I do, too—and more.) The varied response to the column showed me that while everything changes around us, we need to believe in something. There remains a sense that we are being swept through time by events and circumstances over which we have no control, but are also buoyed by the intuition that if we could somehow do the right thing, right now, the world would be a better place.

Call it science. Call it the wisdom of the ages. Call it luck. Call it God, by whatever name humans over the centuries have chosen.

I call it God, who goes on forever.

ACKNOWLEDGMENTS

In order to thank the people who helped make this book possible, I could simply provide my lists of email contacts, Facebook friends, refrigerator-door phone list, and my much-scribbled-upon address book. At the risk of sounding like a Juno winner, I'd like to acknowledge the contributions of everyone, because you are all part of my life experience which influenced what I have written here.

Specifically, though, I'd like to thank my mother, Mary, and my late father, Percy, to whom I have dedicated this book. They urged me to push the limits of my understanding while I was yet a child and to feel free to question everything. I thank my brothers for forcing me to continually live up to my valued position as their big sister (and their wives for freeing me from that responsibility!).

I am grateful for my husband's wacky sense of humour, which helps me look at the world sideways, for his constant encouragement to keep on keeping on, and for supporting my crackpot ideas and projects as well as the good ones. My children and their families are oases of common sense, twenty-first-century wisdom, and new insights.

My friends are amazing—there is no other word. I owe special thanks to Cathe MacLean for clipping every single column I ever wrote and saving them so I could write a book someday, and to Sheree Fitch for pushing and dragging me to the finish line.

To the *Chronicle Herald*: thank you for letting my voice be heard.

To Patrick, Whitney, Emily, Heather, Debbie, Terrilee, and everyone else at Nimbus: thank you for seeing the possibilities in a book of this nature.

To illustrator Colleen MacIsaac: thank you for encapsulating my concepts so well!

To my cousins, clergy, fitness instructors, fellow writers, club members, and other beloved family, colleagues, friends, and neighbours: thank you. If I went off in a daydream while you were talking to me, know that you contributed something to this book.

Last, and first, I thank God for creating all of you—and me, too. (No, I don't have God's email address. Don't need it.)